Young
Rewired
State_

GET
CODING!

WALKER BOOKS
AND SUBSIDIARIES
LONDON • BOSTON • SYDNEY • AUCKLAND

CONTENTS

ABOUT THIS BOOK

Hello! We're Young Rewired State, a worldwide community of digital-makers aged eighteen and under. We've made this book because we want you to become a technology star of the future. We hope that *Get Coding!* will not only teach you how to code, but also show you how fun and exciting it can be. Coding is one of the most important skills young people can learn and there's never been a better time to master it.

what does this book teach you?

This book teaches you how to code using three essential programming languages: HTML, CSS and JavaScript. A computer can be made to do almost anything, but first someone has to write a program for it to follow. Programs have to be written in languages a computer can understand. Coding is all about learning to write programs in these different languages.

HTML, CSS and JavaScript are three of the most important programming languages in the world. They are used by web developers to build the websites and web-based apps and games you use every day. This book will teach you how to write code and build programs using these programming languages. In this book you will learn real-life coding skills you can use to do all kinds of programming.

Young Rewired State_

Find out more about Young Rewired State:
www.yrs.io   www.getcodingkids.com

Go to
www.getcodingkids.com
for help and support

How does this book work?

There are six chapters in this book. Each chapter contains a mission that will teach you new HTML, CSS and JavaScript coding skills. Your job is to work through the chapters and use your skills to complete the missions. You will be joining Professor Bairstone, Dr Day and Ernest, who need your help to keep a valuable diamond safe.

Prof. Bairstone

Dr Day

Hello! Great to meet you!

Ernest

What do you need?

All you need is a computer (PC or Mac) that is connected to the Internet.

We hope you enjoy this book and it inspires you to get coding!

Tweet us: **@youngrewired #GetCoding**
Also find us on YouTube, Facebook and Instagram

INTRODUCTION:
COMPUTER CODING

Computers are an important part of our lives today.
We use them all the time to do many different things.
You've probably used a laptop, desktop computer
or tablet before. But did you know
that a smartphone is also a computer?
And that there are computers inside cash machines, washing
machines, games consoles and cars? All these computers
look different and work slightly differently, but all have
one thing in common: they have to follow sets of
instructions, called programs, to complete tasks.

Perfect programming

Computers are electronic devices that can process
information. They can be the size of a room or fit
inside tiny gadgets, and do all kinds of complex tasks.
Computers are made up of hardware (the physical
parts of a computer you can touch) and software
(the parts you can't touch). Computers need software
because they can't think or act by themselves. They
have to follow a detailed series of commands in a
piece of software known as a program. Programs are
written in programming languages that computers can
understand. Writing programs is therefore known as
coding or programming. You can write programs
to do all sorts of things. You might have used some
of these:

- Facebook
- Google
- iTunes
- Microsoft Word
- Minecraft
- YouTube

You use programs every day. When you check your friend's profile on Facebook, send a text, use a microwave or play a DVD, you're using computer programs. In fact, you can write a program to make a computer do almost anything. The people who write programs are called programmers or software developers. Programmers write code in different programming languages depending on the type of program they want to build.

Programming languages

There are many different programming languages you can code in. Computers can understand more than one programming language at a time, so programs are often written using several different programming languages. A programmer's job is to pick the best languages for the program they are building because different programming languages work better for different things. Every programming language has things it's good and bad at. Some commonly used programming languages are listed below.

- ♥ **C** and **C++** are used to build operating systems for your computer.

- ♥ **C#**, **Java**, **PHP** and **Ruby** are used to build websites.

- ♥ **C#**, **Java** and **Objective-C** are used to write **apps** for computers and smartphones.

- ♥ **SQL** is used to extract information from databases.

You may have already done some coding at school, using programming languages such as Scratch or Python. Scratch is made up of coloured blocks of code that you drag and drop together to create programs. It's great for making small games and animations. Python is a text-based programming language, which means you create programs by typing out each instruction for your computer as a piece of code. Programs like Instagram are written in Python.

In this book you are going to learn how to write code using three programming languages: HTML, CSS and JavaScript. Using these programming languages, you are going to create programs that run on the Internet. You are going to create a website, app, game and many other programs that will run in your web browser.

CODE WORDS An **APP** (**APPLICATION**) is a type of computer program. Apps are usually programs that a user needs to perform specific tasks, like word processing or emailing.

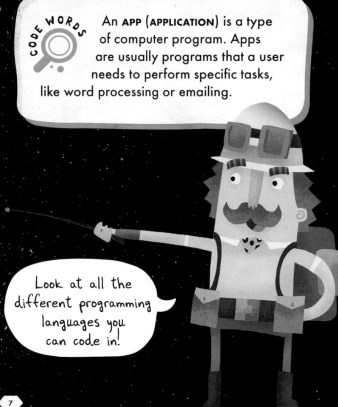

Look at all the different programming languages you can code in!

CODING AND THE WEB

A giant network connects lots of computers all over the world. This network is called the Internet and it allows us to access and share information with people around the world in seconds. You've probably used the Internet to visit websites, watch videos, send emails, listen to music or play games. But did you know that when you connect to the Internet and view a website you are using a chain of different computer programs? Programs on our computers called web browsers connect via Internet networks to programs running on web servers, letting us share information quickly and easily.

World Wide Web

The Internet is made up of lots of smaller networks. The World Wide Web (or "the web") is a network connecting many of our computers, used daily by millions of people. The web is made up of lots of individual web pages.

A web page is a file written in computer code by a programmer. Web pages are nearly all written in the same programming language, which is called HTML. HTML contains the information your computer needs to display a web page on-screen. When a group of web pages is linked together, the group of pages is called a website. You access web pages using a program called a web browser.

Web browsers

Web browsers are computer programs that allow us to view web pages. You have probably come across web browsers such as Google Chrome, Microsoft Internet Explorer, Safari and Mozilla Firefox, and used them to access all sorts of different websites. Your web browser uses a web address to find the web page you want on the web. It then accesses the information for the web page using another program, called a web server.

Professor Bairstone is always online, sending emails!

Web servers

Servers are computers that provide other computers with information. A web server can either be hardware (a computer) or software (a program) that helps to deliver a web page to your browser. To access a web page, your web browser has to connect to that page's web server. The program running on the web server then finds the web page your browser has requested. It then sends the web page to your computer as HTML code.

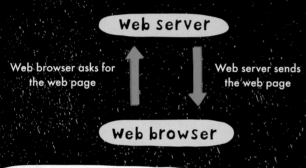

Web server

Web browser asks for the web page

Web server sends the web page

Web browser

Web addresses

Web addresses, or URLs as they are more commonly known, are a handy way for a web browser to find the web server and HTML file it needs on the web. There are millions of websites on the Internet, and if each web page didn't have an individual URL your web browser wouldn't know where to look for it. URLs are split into different parts, each telling your web browser a different piece of information:

This tells the web browser to connect to a web server

This tells the server to send your web browser a HTML file

http://www.getcodingkids.com/hello.html

This tells the web browser which server to connect to

Web pages

When the web server sends your web browser a web page, it sends the information in a HTML document. HTML documents are made up of HTML elements, such as text and images, as well as exact instructions for the browser about how to display and position the elements on-screen.

When a web browser reads the instructions in the HTML code, we say the browser "parses" the HTML document. As it parses and decodes the instructions, the browser draws each element of the document on-screen. A HTML document could contain just a few words of text. The simplest HTML document is only a few lines of code long and looks like this:

```
<!DOCTYPE html>
<html>          HTML element
<head>
    <title>Get Coding!</title>
</head>
<body>
    Are you ready to get coding?
</body>
</html>
```

Or the document might be more complicated, containing other programming languages as well, such as CSS and JavaScript.

Turn over to find out more about HTML and the other programming languages used to code web pages!

CODING WEB PAGES

The three most common programming languages in the world are HTML, CSS and JavaScript. These languages are used to build web pages and web-based apps. Using them together allows you to build web pages that not only look great, but are interactive too. In this book you are going to learn how to code in these languages.

HTML

Today, nearly all web pages are written using HTML (HyperText Markup Language) code. HTML was developed by Tim Berners-Lee in the early 1990s. HTML is a great way of creating the basic structure of your web page. HTML documents are made up of individual HTML elements. Elements are created using opening and closing tags. Each tag is the name of the element enclosed in angle brackets (< >). The content goes between the tags. Each HTML tag is an instruction to your web browser, telling it how to show the content on your screen. Tags allow you to add text, images and videos to your web page and divide information into sections, such as lines or paragraphs.

CSS

CSS (Cascading Style Sheets) is a programming language that works with HTML to make your web page look good. HTML looks very boring on its own, so you use CSS to change the colour, font and position of text and images. CSS will let you make a piece of text bigger or smaller, change your background colour or position an image in the centre of a page.

JavaScript

JavaScript is a very important programming language because it brings web pages to life by making them interactive. An interactive web page changes when the user does something. So if you want your user to be able to click a button, or an alert to pop up, you need to use JavaScript. If you use HTML and CSS without JavaScript, you will have a web page that looks great but doesn't respond to the user.

SOME CLEVER CODERS

Ada Lovelace (1815–52) wrote the world's first computer program in 1843.

Grace Hopper (1906–92) created the world's first computer compiler, a program that turns human-readable code into computer code.

Tim Berners-Lee (1955–) is a computer scientist who invented the World Wide Web and the HTML programming language.

Alan Turing (1912–54) was a mathematician who established the foundations of modern computer science.

Paul Allen (1953–) and **Bill Gates** (1955–) founded the Microsoft technology company and created the Microsoft Windows operating system.

Brendan Eich (1961–) created the JavaScript programming language.

Markus Persson (1979–) is a computer game programmer who created Minecraft.

Sergey Brin (1973–) and **Larry Page** (1973–) are computer scientists and Internet entrepreneurs who co-founded the Google search engine.

Mark Zuckerberg (1984–) is a computer programmer and Internet entrepreneur, who co-founded Facebook.

These are very brainy people!

HOW TO USE THIS BOOK

There are six exciting missions in *Get Coding!* Your job is to work through each mission and learn how to code in HTML, CSS and JavaScript. You can then use your new coding skills to help the intrepid explorer Professor Bairstone and top scientist Dr Day, who are in urgent need of your assistance. They have found the valuable Monk Diamond on an expedition and need your help to keep it safe.

Mission Briefs

At the start of each mission you will receive a Mission Brief from Professor Bairstone or Dr Day. The brief will ask you to use your coding knowledge to help with a Do It Yourself Task. The tasks include building a web page, creating a password, coding an app, planning a route, making a game and building a finished website.

The Explorer's Encyclopedia

You will find out more about Professor Bairstone, Dr Day and the Monk Diamond in the entries from the Explorer's Encyclopedia after the briefs. You can use this information to help you complete the tasks.

The Monk Diamond

Code Skills

The best way to learn how to code is through practice! At first coding can seem daunting as you have to use special words and symbols. But you will soon become familiar with the ways the different programming languages have to be written. To help you see how each new piece of code works you will find Code Skills exercises dotted throughout each mission. Follow the step-by-step instructions in each exercise and master a new Code Skill every time.

Do It Yourself Tasks

At the end of each mission is a Do It Yourself Task. Use the code you have learnt in the Code Skills to complete the tasks and accomplish the missions. The future of the Monk Diamond is in your hands!

KEY CODE SKILLS

Before you receive the brief for Mission 1, there are some basic Code Skills you need to learn. You will use these skills throughout the entire book, so it's important to get to grips with them now. You can code using a PC or a Mac, but you have to create and save your HTML file in a different way depending on which system you are using.

KEY CODE SKILL 1 ► CREATING A FOLDER

You need to have a place in your computer where you can save all your HTML files. Make a folder on your desktop called **Coding**. It's really important that you save all your HTML files in the same place, so make sure you keep using this folder as you work through the missions.

PC	On a PC, right-click on your desktop and click *New* and then *Folder*. Call your new folder **Coding**.
Mac	On a Mac, hold down the *Control* key and click on your desktop. Then select *New Folder*. Call your new folder **Coding**.

Master these essential Code Skills and you'll be ready for the first mission!

KEY CODE SKILL 2 ► CREATING A HTML FILE

You need to know how to create a HTML file so you can write code. Programmers normally use specialist software to write code, but all computers come with text-editing programs that let you write HTML files. If you have a PC, you can use Notepad. If you have a Mac, you can use TextEdit.

PC

On a PC, you'll find Notepad by going into the *Start* menu and typing it in the search bar.

Mac

On a Mac, you'll find TextEdit by typing it in the *Spotlight* search magnifying glass in the top-right of your screen. When you open TextEdit, you need to do the following things:
- Set up your file as a plain text (rather than rich text) file. To do this go to *Format* in the menu bar and select *Make Plain Text*.
- Also go to *TextEdit* in the menu bar. Select *Preferences*. In the *New Document* tab in the *Format* section, make sure *Plain text* is checked. In the *Options* section, make sure *Smart quotes* is unchecked.
- In the *Open and Save* tab in *Preferences,* make sure *Display HTML files as HTML* code *instead of formatted text* is checked.

KEY CODE SKILL 3 ► SAVING YOUR HTML FILE

When you save your HTML file for the first time, you need to make sure you save it using the file extension **.html** at the end of your file name. Your computer uses file extensions to work out how to open files. By giving your file the extension **.html** you're telling your computer that it should open it in a web browser.

PC

On a PC, you need to:
- Go to *File* and select *Save As*.
- Select the **Coding** folder as the destination to save the file to.
- Choose a name for your file, such as Mission1, and type it into the *File name* bar.
- After the name of the file, type **.html** so your file name reads **Mission1.html**. Click *Save*.

Mac

On a Mac, you need to:
- Go to *File* and select *Save*.
- Select your **Coding** folder as the destination to save your file to.
- Choose a name for your file, such as Mission1, and type it into the *Save As* bar.
- After the name of the file, type **.html** so your file name reads **Mission1.html**.
- Make sure the check box *If no extension is provided, use ".txt".* is unchecked. Click *Save*.

KEY CODE SKILL 4 ▶ OPENING YOUR HTML FILE

To see your code displayed on-screen, you need to open your HTML file in a web browser. You then might want to go back into your text-editing program to make some changes to your code.

PC

On a PC, you need to:
- Save your file, as described in Key Code Skill 3.
- Open your **Coding** folder on your desktop. Double-click on your HTML file. It will open in your web browser.
- When you want to edit your code, right-click on the HTML file in your **Coding** folder. Select *Open with* and choose Notepad.

Mac

On a Mac, you need to:
- Save your file, as described in Key Code Skill 3.
- Open your **Coding** folder on your desktop. Double-click on your HTML file. It will open in your web browser.
- When you want to edit your code, right-click on the HTML file in your **Coding** folder. Select *Open with* and choose TextEdit.

> Use a web browser like Mozilla Firefox or Google Chrome.

KEY CODE SKILL 5 ▶ USING THE *GET CODING!* WEBSITE

Don't forget that as you work through the book you can use the *Get Coding!* website to help you with your missions. You'll find entries from the Explorer's Encyclopedia and images that you can use. If you get stuck at any point when you're writing code, go to the website and see what your code block should look like. You can even copy and paste the code blocks from the website into your text-editing program.

The *Get Coding!* URL is **www.getcodingkids.com**

On the website you will find:
- Professor Bairstone's entries on the Explorer's Encyclopedia
- Pictures of Professor Bairstone, Ernest, Dr Day and the Monk Diamond
- Code blocks for each Code Skills exercise and Do It Yourself Task.

> Some of these steps may vary depending on the system you're using. If you're having trouble, do an online search for how to write HTML in the version of the program you're using.

BUILD A WEB PAGE

- ◆ LEARN WHAT HTML IS AND HOW IT WORKS

- ◆ MAKE A SIMPLE WEB PAGE USING HTML

- ◆ ADD TEXT AND IMAGES TO YOUR HTML WEB PAGE

- ◆ LEARN HOW TO LAY OUT AND DESIGN YOUR WEB PAGE USING CSS

Mission Brief

Dear Coder,

We haven't met before, but I'm sure you already know my name. I'm the famous explorer, Professor Harry Bairstone. I'm emailing you because I am in desperate need of your help.

I am currently on an expedition in the mountains of Siberia, with the top scientist Dr Ruby Day and my dog Ernest. The aim of our expedition was to find prehistoric fossils. Instead we have made an even more sensational discovery.

We were exploring a cave when Ernest suddenly started barking and sniffing at a large boulder. We looked closer and saw that something had been hidden in a crack in the rock-face. Dr Day pulled out the object. It was a small box, wrapped in oilcloth. When I opened the box, I couldn't believe my eyes.

It was the legendary Monk Diamond! As I'm sure you know, the Monk Diamond was stolen from Moscow three years ago in a daring robbery and its whereabouts has been unknown until now. Our discovery is of great international significance.

We can only access the Internet briefly, using my emergency booster pack. Dr Day and I were hoping you could help us by using your Code Skills to build a web page about our exciting discovery.

I'm attaching an entry from the Explorer's Encyclopedia, which will tell you all about the Monk Diamond's remarkable history. You can use the information to build your web page. We will use the page to announce our discovery to the world the moment we arrive in Moscow.

Thank you for helping us with this exciting mission. It's going to be great!

Warmest wishes from the chilly mountains,
Professor Harry Bairstone

The Monk Diamond

From the Explorer's Encyclopedia, the guide to every adventure

THE EXPLORER'S
ENCYCLOPEDIA
The Guide to Every Adventure

Home page
Contents
Featured discoveries
Famous explorers
Historical expeditions

This entry is about the Monk Diamond. For other jewels, see Diamonds.

The **Monk Diamond** is one of the rarest and most precious <u>diamonds</u> in the world, famous for its distinctive green colour. It was discovered in 1880 and was bought by a Russian nobleman for his wife in 1889.

During the <u>Russian Revolution</u>, the Monk Diamond was stolen from the nobleman's palace in <u>St Petersburg</u>. For the next 30 years, the Monk Diamond's whereabouts

Professor Bairstone's Fact File

The Monk Diamond

Age:	over 1 billion years old
Colour:	Green
Cut:	Oval
Carats:	300
Clarity:	Flawless
Value:	over £10 million

was unknown. In 1947 it was discovered during a police raid on a gang of petty criminals in Moscow. It was returned to the nobleman's family.

The nobleman's son decided the Monk Diamond was unlucky and sold it to the House of Volkov, Moscow's oldest jewellery house. The House of Volkov paid an undisclosed sum for the jewel, but it was rumoured to be the most expensive diamond sale ever.

The Monk Diamond was on display in the House of Volkov's private collection until three years ago, when it was stolen in an audacious raid. Despite a long investigation and the promise of a huge reward, the police were unable to track down the culprits and the case remains unsolved.

The thieves are believed to be the Bond Brothers, the international gang of jewel thieves responsible for numerous high profile thefts. A theory put forward by the explorer Professor Bairstone is that the Monk Diamond was smuggled out of Moscow by the Bond Brothers and hidden somewhere in Russia. He thinks "the thieves are biding their time until they can sell the diamond on the black market without attracting suspicion."

CODING WITH HTML

Now you've read the Mission Brief, it's time to get coding. To build Professor Bairstone's web page, you're first going to need to learn to write HTML (HyperText Markup Language). HTML is the programming language used by programmers to build websites. It allows you to give your browser instructions. You use HTML to add text and images to a web page. You also use it to group together pieces of information into lines, paragraphs or sections.

A HTML web page is called a document. It's made up of HTML elements. Elements are created using small pieces of code called tags. Tags nearly always come in pairs and surround every piece of content (like a piece of text or an image) on the page. Each tag contains an instruction for your web browser, telling it how to show the element on-screen. This is why HTML is called a "markup language". You use tags to mark up each piece of content with an instruction for your browser.

HTML tags

Each tag is made up of a piece of code surrounded by two angle brackets (< >). The angle brackets are on the same keys as the full stop and comma symbols on your keyboard. Let's look at an example of a tag:

It's simple: <p> is code for paragraph. You'll learn more about this tag later in the mission.

```
<p>Professor Bairstone and Dr Day have discovered the Monk Diamond.</p>
```

Opening tag   Closing tag

This is the paragraph <p> tag. When tags come in pairs, we call the first tag the opening tag and the second tag the closing tag. You can spot a closing tag because it contains a forward slash (/). When your browser reads this code it understands that you are telling it to group the text between the opening and closing <p> tags into a paragraph.

To code a web page you have to create a HTML file in a text-editing program. Your browser expects some tags to appear in a certain order. You need to code the tags that contain instructions about the whole page first. Then you code the tags with instructions for specific pieces of content on your page. Tags can be put inside other tags. You just have to remember to close each tag when you've finished with it.

Let's have a look at the HTML tags you need to code a very simple web page. If you use these tags you will create a web page that is made up of a title and some text. Each tag gives your browser a different piece of information:

`<!DOCTYPE html>`

This is called the <!DOCTYPE> declaration and it is always the first line of a HTML file. It tells our browser what version of HTML our page has been coded in. It is not a HTML tag so it is written with capital letters and it doesn't need a closing tag.

`<html>`

This is the <html> tag and it tells the browser that we have used HTML to code our page.

`<head>`

This is the <head> tag. Inside are pieces of content that aren't displayed in the main <body> of your page, like the title. You can also put instructions that you want your browser to apply to your whole page here.

```
<!DOCTYPE html>
<html>
<head>
    <title>
        The Monk Diamond Discovery
    </title>
</head>
<body>
    <p>Professor Bairstone and Dr Day have
        discovered the Monk Diamond.</p>
</body>
</html>
```

`<title>`

The <title> tag goes inside the <head> tag. The content between the tags will not appear in the main body of our page. It will be the title of the browser window when you open the page in your browser.

`<body>`

All the content you want to see displayed in your web page goes inside the <body> tag. So this text about the Monk Diamond will appear on our page when we open the file in our web browser.

`<p>`

This is the paragraph tag. All the text between the opening and closing tags will be grouped into a paragraph.

Turn over to see what this code will look like on-screen in our web browser!

When we save the code we wrote in our text-editing program and then open it in our web browser, our browser decodes our HTML file and draws on-screen a web page that looks like this:

The Monk Diamond Di ✖

Professor Bairstone and Dr Day have discovered the Monk Diamond.

See how the text between the opening and closing <title> tags has become the title of the browser window?

Look at how all the text between the opening and closing <p> tags has become the contents of your web page!

Writing HTML

Now you know what HTML tags are and how they work, it's time for you to have a go at using them. The best way to learn new pieces of code is to practise writing them. Throughout this book you will find Code Skills. Follow the step-by-step instructions in the exercises and learn new skills each time.

It's really important to make sure your code is as accurate as possible. Having a letter or a symbol wrong or missing could stop your code from working, as your browser won't be able to understand your instructions. If you are having problems making a program work, it's a good idea to check the following things:

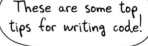

- ♦ That you've not missed out any tags or used them in the wrong order
- ♦ That there are no typos or spelling errors in your code
- ♦ That you've used correct capitalization throughout your code
- ♦ That you've included all the symbols you need, in the right order
- ♦ That you're using straight quotes (" ") and not curly quotes (" ")
- ♦ That you've closed all your tags by including the forward slash (/)
- ♦ That your text-editing program has saved your file as a HTML file (**.html**)

These are some top tips for writing code!

If you're still stuck, go to the *Get Coding!* website (**www.getcodingkids.com**) where you will be able to copy and paste the code block you need.

CODE SKILLS ► WRITING HTML

Let's use HTML tags to code a very simple web page. Follow these steps to learn how to structure a HTML web page that is made up of a title and a piece of text.

1. Open up your text-editing program. Look back at Key Code Skill 2 on page 14 if you need a reminder about how to do this.

2. Type this code into your text-editing program:

```
<!DOCTYPE html>
<html>
<head>
   <title>The Monk Diamond</title>
</head>
<body>
   <p>The Monk Diamond is a rare jewel.</p>
</body>
</html>
```

Make sure you copy the code carefully. Your web browser won't be able to read your code if there are any mistakes in it. The <!DOCTYPE> declaration has to have capital letters and your last tag always has to be </html>. Check you have closed each tag by including the forward slash (/).

3. Save your file in your **Coding** folder as a HTML file (**.html**). Call it **webpagetemplate.html**. Go back to Key Code Skills 1 and 3 on pages 13 and 14 if you need a reminder about how to do this.

4. Open your HTML file in your web browser. See Key Code Skill 4 on page 15 if you need a reminder about how to do this. Your code will be displayed on-screen as a web page, like this:

The Monk Diamond is a rare jewel.

Then open your file in your text-editing program again. Change the text between the opening and closing <title> tags and <p> tags to text of your choice. Save your file.

5. Press the *Refresh* button in your browser. On a PC, press *F5*. On a Mac, press *Command+R*. Your changes to the text will appear on-screen.

You just built your first web page!

Let's try coding paragraphs and line breaks in a web page, using the <p> and <br/> tags.

1. Open up your text-editing program. Create a new HTML file called **breaks.html**. Check the Key Code Skills on pages 13–15 if you need a reminder about how to do this. Then copy and paste your code from **webpagetemplate.html** into your new file. Modify the code so that it looks like this:

```
<!DOCTYPE html>
<html>
<head>
   <title>The Monk Diamond</title>
</head>
<body>
</body>
</html>
```

2. Use the paragraph <p> tag. Open the <p> tag, type some text, then use the closing </p> tag. Repeat as many times as you want. Your code will look like this:

```
<body>
   <p>The Monk Diamond has been
      discovered in Siberia.</p>
   <p>Ernest, Professor Bairstone's
      dog, found the jewel.</p>
</body>
```

Great work! But what about some pictures of the Monk Diamond?

3. Type some more text in your first paragraph. Add the line break <br/> tag to the end of a line of text like this:

```
<body>
   <p>The Monk Diamond has been
      discovered in Siberia.<br/>
      Professor Bairstone
      and Dr Day were on a fossil-
      finding expedition.</p>
   <p>Ernest, Professor Bairstone's
      dog, found the jewel.</p>
</body>
```

4. Save your HTML file in your **Coding** folder. Then open your web page in your browser. Your page will look like this:

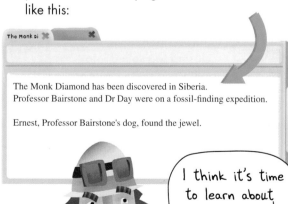

The Monk Diamond has been discovered in Siberia.
Professor Bairstone and Dr Day were on a fossil-finding expedition.

Ernest, Professor Bairstone's dog, found the jewel.

I think it's time to learn about the image tag!

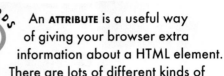

The image tag: `<img/>`

Now you've mastered the paragraph and line break tags, let's learn how to add an image to our web page. The image `<img/>` tag is another self-closing tag. Inside the tag itself you have to include a piece of information called the source (src) **attribute**. An image tag looks like this:

```
<img src="image.jpg"/>
```

The equals sign (=) and double quotes (" ") set the value of the source attribute

You have to include the source attribute in the `<img/>` tag so your browser knows where to find your image. Without it your browser won't know what to display on-screen. The value of your source attribute can either be set to a file name of a saved image or a URL (web address) of your image.

CODE WORDS An **ATTRIBUTE** is a useful way of giving your browser extra information about a HTML element. There are lots of different kinds of attributes you can include in your tags.

There are two parts to an attribute: the attribute name and the value of the attribute. You use an equals sign (=) to set the value of the attribute and put the value in double quotes (" "). So an attribute will always look like this: name="value". Attributes are added to the opening tag, or to the only tag (in the case of a self-closing tag).

Using a saved image

If you have an image saved as a JPEG file (**.jpg**) in your **Coding** folder, it's really easy to add this image to your page. All you need to do is set the value of the source attribute to the name of your image file, using the equals sign (=) and double quotes (" "). So if your file is called **diamond.jpg**, your code will look like this:

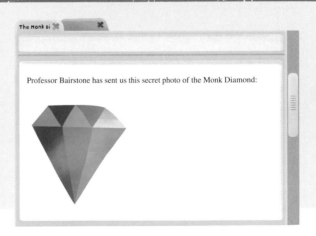

The Monk Di

Professor Bairstone has sent us this secret photo of the Monk Diamond:

```
<body>
    <p>Professor Bairstone has sent us this secret photo of the Monk Diamond:</p>
    <img src="diamond.jpg"/>
</body>
```

Image tag

Source attribute

File name

27

Using an image URL

If there's an image on the Internet you want to use on your web page, you have to set the value of the source attribute in your `<img/>` tag to the URL of the image. You find the URL of a picture by right-clicking on it and selecting *Copy image URL* on a PC or *Copy image address* on a Mac. You then paste the URL inside your `<img/>` tag as the value of the source attribute. Don't forget to put it in double quotes (" "), like this:

```
<body>
    <p>This is Professor Bairstone and Dr Day's first expedition together.</p>
    <p>Here is a photo of the team:</p>
    <img src="https://getcodingkids.com/team_photo.jpg"/>
</body>
```

A URL will always start with http:// or https://

The Monk D

This is Professor Bairstone and Dr Day's first expedition together.
Here is a photo of the team:

Naming an image

If you include an image on your page, you should always give it a name. It helps search engines like Google find your page. A name is also handy for users who may not be able to download images.

To name your image, you need to add the alternative (alt) attribute after your source attribute, like this:

```
<img src="diamond.jpg" alt="Diamond"/>
```

Alternative attribute

The complete code block for our web page with text and images now looks like this:

```
<body>
    <p>This is Professor Bairstone and Dr Day's first expedition together.</p>
    <p>Here is a photo of the team:</p>
    <img src="https://getcodingkids.com/team_photo.jpg" alt="The Team"/>
</body>
```

In some web browsers, if you hover your mouse over the image in your browser and leave it still, a little pop-up will be displayed containing the text in your alt attribute

Did you notice?

The quotes in our code are always straight (" ") rather than curly (" "). Your browser won't understand instructions if they are in curly quotes.

CODE SKILLS ► ADDING IMAGES

Let's have a go at adding some images of the Monk Diamond, Professor Bairstone, Dr Day and Ernest to our web page to make it look more exciting.

1. Go to the images section of the *Get Coding!* website. Find the image of the Monk Diamond. Right-click on the image and select *Save Image As*. Save the image as a JPEG file (**.jpg**) in your **Coding** folder. Call it **diamond.jpg**.

2. Open up your text-editing program and create a new HTML file called **images.html**. Then copy and paste your code from **webpagetemplate.html** into your new file. Modify the code so that it looks like this:

```
<!DOCTYPE html>
<html>
<head>
   <title>The Monk Diamond</title>
</head>
<body>
   <p>The Monk Diamond is a rare
      green colour.</p>
</body>
</html>
```

3. Now add an image of the Monk Diamond to your page. Add an <img/> tag with an empty source attribute after your closing </p> tag, like this:

```
<p>The Monk Diamond is a rare green
   colour.</p>
<img src=" "/>
```

4. Then add a value to the source attribute. Add the name of the image file you saved in your **Coding** folder, like this:

```
<p>The Monk Diamond is a rare green
   colour.</p>
<img src="diamond.jpg"/>
```

 Save your HTML file and open it in your browser. Your image will be displayed on-screen.

5. Now add an image of Professor Bairstone, Dr Day and Ernest to your page using a URL. Add another paragraph and an <img/> tag with an empty source attribute, like this:

```
<p>The Monk Diamond is a rare green
   colour.</p>
<img src="diamond.jpg"/>
<p>The team was delighted with their
   discovery.</p>
<img src=" "/>
```

Don't forget that attributes always have to be in double quotes.

PTO ➡

CODING WITH CSS

So far in this mission you've been coding using HTML. As you've just seen, `<div>` tags are used to group together HTML elements so you can easily change them. To change the look and position of your HTML elements, you have to use CSS.

CSS is a programming language often used with HTML. It is used by programmers to change the way HTML elements look when they're displayed in your browser. CSS is short for Cascading Style Sheets and is sometimes called "style sheets" or "styles". You can use CSS to change the design of your page by adding colours or changing the size and shape of HTML elements. You can also use CSS to change where things are positioned. In fact, there are many different things you can do with CSS to change the look and feel of your page.

The style attribute

To use CSS to change a HTML element you can add a style attribute to your opening HTML tag. You can use the style attribute with any HTML tag. The style attribute works in exactly the same way as the source and alt attributes we used earlier in the mission. Let's have a look at how we add a style attribute:

```
<p style="CSS-property: value;">The Monk Diamond had been hidden in a cave.</p>
```

Style attribute   CSS

Just like we saw earlier, the value of our style attribute is set using the equals sign (=) and enclosed in double quotes (" "). We apply CSS to our HTML tag by setting the value of the style attribute to CSS. CSS is a very simple programming language to write. It's always split into two parts: a property and a value.

CSS properties and values

When you write CSS you always have to use both a property and a value. The property tells your browser what part of the HTML element you want to change. The value tells your browser exactly what to change it to. So it works like this:

CSS	What does it mean?	Example values
property	The thing you want to change	background-color; height;
value	What you want to change it to	red; 200px;

When you use CSS you divide the property from the value by inserting a colon (:). At the end of the value, you use a semi-colon (;). If the CSS is more than one word, you join the two words using a hyphen (-). If you don't use the right **syntax**, your browser won't be able to decode your instructions. Your style attribute should always be written like this:

```
style="CSS-property: value;"
```

Hyphen   Colon   Semi-colon

CODE WORDS

SYNTAX is the set of rules which decide the way a programming language is structured and written.

Your browser has hundreds of different built-in CSS properties and values that you can use in your HTML tags to change your page.

Let's take a closer look at how we can use CSS with <div> tags. If we want to change the background colour of a section of our page, we can use CSS and HTML like this:

Look at how we can use HTML and CSS together to change our page!

Style attribute   CSS property   CSS value

```
<body>
  <div style="background-color: green;">
   <p>The Monk Diamond had been hidden in a cave.</p>
   <p>It was inside a crack in the rock.</p>
  </div>
</body>
```

Did you notice?

All words in CSS are spelt using American English. If you don't use American English, your browser won't understand your CSS. For example, every time you write the word "colour", you must use the American spelling, which is "color".

The Monk Di

The Monk Diamond had been hidden in a cave.

It was inside a crack in the rock.

The background-color CSS property

Now you understand more about CSS and how it works, let's see how we can use CSS properties to make our page more colourful. Professor Bairstone and Dr Day's discovery is sure to be an international sensation and our web page needs to look eye-catching and interesting.

We can change the background colour of different areas of our page using different <div> tags. First we have to add style attributes to each of our opening <div> tags. Then inside the style attribute we set the background-color CSS property and choose a colour for the CSS value. The code we need looks like this:

```
<body>
    <p>THE STOLEN MONK DIAMOND IS DISCOVERED!</p>
    <div style="background-color: green;">
        <p>Professor Bairstone, Dr Day and Ernest were on an expedition.<br/>
            They made an exciting discovery in the mountains.</p>
    </div>
    <div style="background-color: cyan;">
        <p>Ernest started sniffing and barking at a rock in a cave.<br/>
            Hidden inside the rock was the Monk Diamond.</p>
    </div>
</body>
```

Background-color property

The Monk Di

THE STOLEN MONK DIAMOND IS DISCOVERED!

Professor Bairstone, Dr Day and Ernest were on an expedition.
They made an exciting discovery in the mountains.

Ernest started sniffing and barking at a rock in a cave.
Hidden inside the rock was the Monk Diamond.

This is such a good Code Skill to learn.

Did you notice?

There are thousands of colours that you can use as values in CSS. Go to www.w3schools.com/cssref/css_colornames.asp to view more of them.

CODE SKILLS ▶ WRITING CSS

It's time for you to start using CSS with HTML. Have a go at adding the style attribute to a HTML tag and then setting a CSS property and value.

1. Open up your text-editing program and create a new HTML file called **CSS.html**. Then copy and paste your code from **divs.html** into your new file. Modify the code so that it looks like this:

```
<!DOCTYPE html>
<html>
<head>
   <title>The Monk Diamond</title>
</head>
<body>
   <div>
      <p>The jewel was stolen from Moscow.</p>
      <p>The theft happened three years ago.</p>
   </div>
   <div>
      <p>The Bond Brothers are the prime suspects.</p>
   </div>
</body>
</html>
```

2. Now add an empty style attribute to each of your opening <div> tags, like this:

```
<div style=" ">
```

3. Then add the background-color CSS property to the style attributes. Remember you need to separate the property name and the value with a colon (:). Don't forget the semi-colon (;) at the end of the value. Your opening <div> tags will look like this:

```
<div style="background-color: pink;">
```

4. Save your HTML file and open it in your browser. Try changing the value of the background-color CSS property to different colours. Save your file and refresh your page to see your changes on-screen.

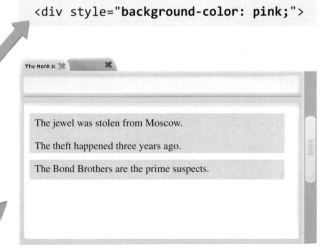

We can also use CSS to position HTML elements, such as `<div>` tags or images, to the left or right of the page. You use the float CSS property and set the value to the left or right.

Float property

```
<body>
  <div style="float: right;">
    The expedition team:<br/>
    <img src="team.jpg" alt="The Team"/>
  </div>
</body>
```

The text-align and float CSS properties are easy ways to create an interesting layout for your web page.

The expedition team:

Using more than one CSS property

You can use more than one CSS property and value in a style attribute. All you have to do is use a semi-colon (;) to separate them. Your browser will read all of the CSS properties and apply them to your HTML element, so you can use as many as you need.

```
<body>
  <div style="background-color: lightblue; float: right;">
    Ernest sniffed out the diamond.
  </div>
</body>
```

Here we've used two CSS properties

The Monk

Ernest sniffed out the diamond.

Look at how we can change both the background colour and position of a `<div>`!

40

Making things different sizes with CSS

We now know how to change the colour of our text, add background colours to our HTML elements and position them in different places on the page. But if we want to make a really interesting web page, we need to know how to change the sizes of our HTML elements. CSS lets us change the size of things really easily. We have to use the width and height CSS properties and set the values to the measurements we want. Let's take a look at how we can use these properties to make a square `<div>`:

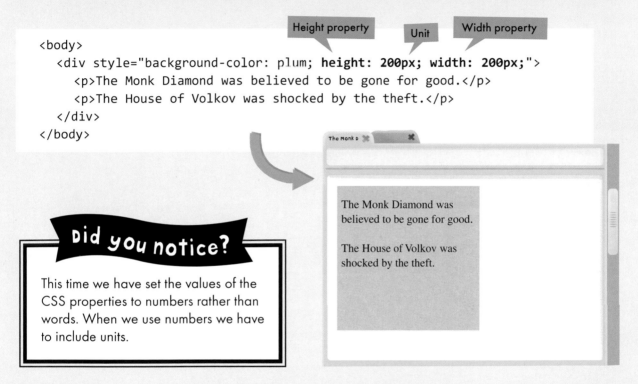

Height property **Unit** **Width property**

```
<body>
    <div style="background-color: plum; height: 200px; width: 200px;">
        <p>The Monk Diamond was believed to be gone for good.</p>
        <p>The House of Volkov was shocked by the theft.</p>
    </div>
</body>
```

The Monk Diamond was believed to be gone for good.

The House of Volkov was shocked by the theft.

Did you notice?

This time we have set the values of the CSS properties to numbers rather than words. When we use numbers we have to include units.

Measurements in CSS

There are lots of different units you can use for measuring in CSS. Make sure you tell your browser what unit you are using by typing it after the number value. Here are some of the most common:

Types of unit:

♥ **Pixels (px)**

♥ **Percentages (%)**

♥ **Points (pt)**

Let's look at how we can use percentages to change the height and width CSS properties of a `<div>`:

```
<body>
  <div style="background-color: palegreen; height: 75%; width: 50%;">
    <p>The police remain baffled by the crime.</p>
    <p>There were no successful leads in the case.</p>
  </div>
</body>
```

Percent value

Did you notice?

When you calculate percentages you are calculating what percentage of the screen you want your element to fill. If you change the size of your browser, the size of the element will also change.

Pixels and points are used in exactly the same way as percentages. With these units, the size of your element will always stay the same, even if you change the size of your browser. Here we've set the height and width CSS properties using values in pixels, and we've used the font-size CSS property to change the size of the text to a value in points.

Pixel value   Pixel value   Point value

```
<body>
  <div style="background-color: gold; height: 200px; width: 350px; font-size: 20pt;">
    <p>The Bond Brothers have never been caught.</p>
  </div>
</body>
```

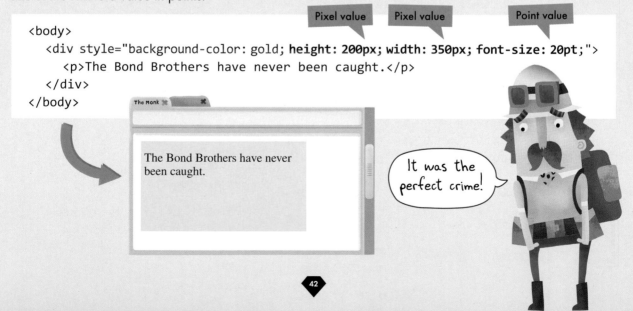

It was the perfect crime!

42

creating borders and space with css

We can also use CSS properties to create borders and space around our HTML elements. To create a border around a HTML element, you have to use the border CSS property and set the values to the width, style and colour you want. Let's look at an example:

Border property   Width   Style   Colour

```
<body>
  <div style="border: 4px solid green; width: 50%; height: 100px;">
    Professor Bairstone and Dr Day are very excited by their discovery.
  </div>
</body>
```

We can also change how much space there is inside a HTML element by using the padding and margin CSS properties. You can set the values for the margin and padding at the top, bottom, left and right of a HTML element. Let's take a look:

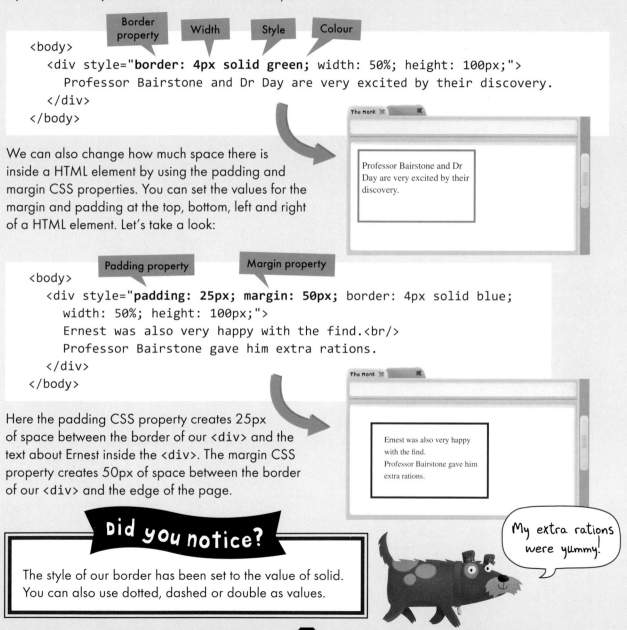

Padding property   Margin property

```
<body>
  <div style="padding: 25px; margin: 50px; border: 4px solid blue;
    width: 50%; height: 100px;">
    Ernest was also very happy with the find.<br/>
    Professor Bairstone gave him extra rations.
  </div>
</body>
```

Here the padding CSS property creates 25px of space between the border of our `<div>` and the text about Ernest inside the `<div>`. The margin CSS property creates 50px of space between the border of our `<div>` and the edge of the page.

Did you notice?

The style of our border has been set to the value of solid. You can also use dotted, dashed or double as values.

My extra rations were yummy!

CODE SKILLS ► USING MORE THAN ONE CSS PROPERTY

There are many different CSS properties you can use to make your web page for Professor Bairstone and Dr Day look great. Now have a go at using more than one CSS property in your code to change the page's layout and design.

1. Open up your text-editing program and create a new HTML file called **CSSproperties.html**. Copy and paste your code from **CSS.html** into your new file and modify it so that there are three `<div>` tags, like this:

```
<!DOCTYPE html>
<html>
<head>
    <title>The Monk Diamond</title>
</head>
<body>
    <div>
        Why was the diamond hidden in a cave?<br/>
        Who hid it there?
    </div>
    <div>
        Was it the Bond Brothers?<br/>
        Could they be watching the cave?
    </div>
    <div>
        Is the team safe?<br/>
        Their camp is very remote.
    </div>
</body>
</html>
```

I really hope we're not in danger!

We have to keep the diamond safe!

2. Change the colour, font size and position of the text in your first `<div>`. Use the color, font-size and text-align CSS properties. Your code will look like this:

```
<div style="color: gray; font-size: 18pt; text-align: center;">
   Why was the diamond hidden in a cave?<br/>
   Who hid it there?
</div>
```

3. Change the width and height of your second `<div>` using the width and height CSS properties. Make your `<div>` 75% of the width of your page and 100px high. Add a background colour and margin to your `<div>` too. Your code will look like this:

```
<div style="width: 75%; height: 100px; background-color: lightblue; margin: 20px;">
   Was it the Bond Brothers?<br/>
   Could they be watching the cave?
</div>
```

4. Let's try moving our third `<div>` to a different position on the page. Use the float CSS property to move your `<div>` to the right of your page. Also add a border and some padding to the `<div>` using the border and padding CSS properties. Your code will look like this:

```
<div style="float: right; border: 6px dotted red; padding: 20px;">
   Is the team safe?<br/>
   Their camp is very remote.
</div>
```

5. Save your HTML file and open it in your browser. Now try changing the values of all the CSS properties to ones of your choice and see what it does to your web page.

Using the class attribute

Applying a CSS class to a HTML element in the <body> of our code is really simple. We just add the name we have chosen for our CSS class to the opening HTML tag for the element we want to change. Rather than using the style attribute, we now use the new class attribute. The class attribute is written and works in exactly the same way as all the other attributes we've used so far in this mission. Let's see what we have to do to apply our CSS class to HTML elements on our page:

```
<!DOCTYPE html>
<html>
<head>
    <title>The Monk Diamond Discovery</title>
    <style>
      .text {
          text-align: center;
          font-size: 18pt;
          background-color: aqua;
      }
    </style>
</head>
<body>
    <p class="text">The Monk Diamond Discovery</p>
    <p>The Monk Diamond has been discovered in the mountains of Siberia.</p>
    <p class="text">The discovery is of great international significance.</p>
    <p>The team were looking for fossils.</p>
    <p class="text">Not one of the world's most famous jewels.</p>
</body>
</html>
```

CSS class

Class attribute

> CSS classes and the class attribute are the best way to write CSS.

In the class attribute we have used our name for the CSS class as the value. We haven't included the dot (.) at the start. As with all the other attributes, we have used an equals sign (=) and double quotes (" ") to set its value. Look at how using a CSS class and the class attribute has easily changed the layout of our page!

The Monk Di

The Monk Diamond Discovery

The Monk Diamond has been discovered in the mountains of Siberia.

The discovery is of great international significance.

The team were looking for fossils.

Not one of the world's most famous jewels.

code skills checklist ✓

CODING WITH CSS

- CSS is always made up of a property and a value. The property is the name of what you want to change and the value is what you want to change it to. There are hundreds of different CSS properties and values.

- You separate the property from the value using a colon (:) and always use a semi-colon (;) after the value. A hyphen (-) is used between words.

- CSS properties and values are always spelt using American English.

- Values can be given in words or numbers. Common units for numerical values include pixels (px), points (pt) and percentages (%).

- You can apply more than one CSS property to a HTML element. The best way to do this is to use a CSS class and the class attribute.

- You tell your browser you are switching from HTML to CSS by using the `<style>` tag. CSS classes are nested inside the `<head>` tag.

- When you choose a CSS class name, it needs to begin with a dot (.). The CSS properties and values you want to apply are put inside curly braces.

- You can apply a CSS class to any HTML element using the class attribute.

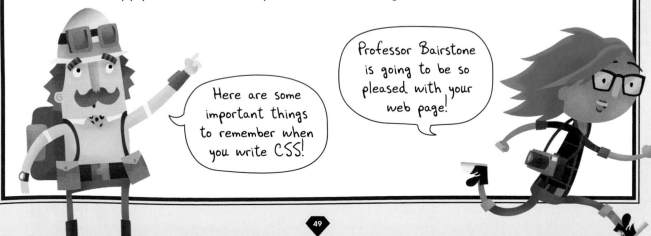

Here are some important things to remember when you write CSS!

Professor Bairstone is going to be so pleased with your web page!

6. Apply your title CSS class to your second `<div>`. Your code will look like this:

```
<div class="title">
    Stolen diamond found on expedition in Siberia!
</div>
```

7. Create a third CSS class in your `<style>` tag and call it body. This CSS class will come after your title CSS class. Set the margin CSS property and value. Your code will look like this:

```
.body {
    margin: 20px;
}
```

8. Apply your body CSS class to your third `<div>`. Your code will look like this:

```
<div class="body">
    Professor Bairstone and Dr Day were looking for fossils in Siberia.<br/>
    They found the stolen diamond hidden inside a remote cave.
</div>
```

9. Save your HTML file and open it in your browser. You will see that each CSS class changes the design of a `<div>`.

Good work! But remember that I was the one who sniffed out the diamond!

More than one CSS class

If you want to make your CSS really effective, it's best to split your CSS classes into groups of CSS properties. This way, when you are designing and laying out a web page you can apply more than one CSS class to your HTML element. It's really easy to use more than one CSS class at a time. All you have to do is add the names of the different classes to your class attribute. Let's take a look:

```
<!DOCTYPE html>
<html>
<head>
   <title>The Monk Diamond</title>
   <style>
     .header {
        background-color: lightgreen;
        width: 70%;
        height: 50%;
     }
     .text {
        text-align: center;
        font-size: 18pt;
     }
     .padding {
        padding: 25px;
     }
   </style>
</head>
<body>
   <div class="header text padding">
     The Monk Diamond<br/>
     An incredible discovery
   </div>
</body>
</html>
```

This is how we add more than one CSS class name to our class attribute

The Monk Diamond
An incredible discovery

Turn over to find out more about the element selector.

Using CSS classes to select HTML elements

Another handy thing you can do with CSS classes is use them to change the CSS properties of a type of HTML element. To do this you use something called the element selector. To use the element selector, you use the name of the element you want to change as the name of your CSS class. You shouldn't include the dot before the name of your CSS class. You also don't need to include a class attribute in the <body>.

So if you want all the text in your paragraphs to be centred and in a certain font size, you can create a CSS class called "p" which will find and select your <p> tags. Let's take a look at what using the element selector does:

```
<!DOCTYPE html>
<html>
<head>
    <title>The Monk Diamond Discovery</title>
    <style>
      p {
          font-size: 16pt;
          text-align: center;
          background-color: lightblue;
      }
    </style>
</head>
<body>
    <p>The Monk Diamond was discovered by Professor Bairstone and Dr Day.</p>
    <p>Ernest alerted them to its hiding place.</p>
    <p>It had been hidden in a crack in the rock.</p>
</body>
</html>
```

The Monk Di

The Monk Diamond was discovered by
Professor Bairstone and Dr Day.

Ernest alerted them to its hiding place.

It had been hidden in a crack in the rock.

Now that's what I call clever coding!

The element selector has changed all our paragraphs without us having to add a class attribute to our <p> tags.

DO IT YOURSELF TASK
BUILD A WEB PAGE

In Mission 1 you learnt lots of HTML and CSS Code Skills. Now it's time to use your new knowledge to build the web page for Professor Bairstone.

The Monk Diamond Discovery Web Page Brief

Build a web page about the discovery of the Monk Diamond. Use HTML and CSS to add text and images and create an interesting design. Include these things on your page:

- **A header banner**
- **A title banner**
- **Text about the Monk Diamond**
- **An image of the team**
- **An image of the diamond**
- **A Monk Diamond fact file**

Save your file in your **Coding** folder and call it **monkdiamonddiscovery.html**.

Turn over to see a code block for a finished web page.

Don't forget to use the Get Coding! website if you get stuck.

This is what your web page would look like if you used this code!

```
<!DOCTYPE html>
<html>
<head>
  <title>The Monk Diamond</title>
  <style>
    body {
      margin: 0px;
    }
    .pad {
      padding: 25px;
    }
    .header {
      background-color: lightblue;
      color: black;
      height: 100px;
      font-size: 36pt;
      text-align: center;
    }
    .welcome {
      background-color: gray;
      color: white;
      font-size: 16pt;
      text-align: center;
      height: 40px;
      margin: 0px;
    }
    .main-text {
      width: 60%;
      float: left;
      background-color: beige;
    }
    .divs {
      margin: 5px;
      width: 25%;
      float: left;
      border: 4px solid lightblue;
    }
  </style>
```

```
    </head>
     <body>
       <div class="header pad">
         The Monk Diamond Discovery
       </div>
       <div>
         <p class="welcome">
           Stolen Diamond Discovered in Siberia!
         </p>
       </div>
       <div class="main-text pad">
         <p>
           Professor Bairstone and Dr Day have made a sensational discovery.<br/>
           They have discovered the Monk Diamond in a remote cave in Siberia.<br/>
           Professor Bairstone's dog, Ernest, sniffed out the diamond.
         </p>
         <p>
           The jewel was stolen three years ago from the House of Volkov.<br/>
           The prime suspects in the theft were the Bond Brothers.<br/>
           The team thinks the diamond had been hidden by the thieves.<br/>
           They sent this photo from their camp:
         </p>
         <img src="team.jpg" alt="The Team" style="height: 150px;"/>
       </div>
       <div class="divs pad">
         <img src="diamond.jpg" alt="Diamond" style="width: 150px;"/>
         <p style="text-align: center;">The Monk Diamond</p>
       </div>
       <div class="divs pad" style="text-align: center;">
         Fact File<br/>
         Carats: 300<br/>
         Colour: Green<br/>
         Value: Over £10 million
       </div>
     </body>
    </html>
```

FUTURE CODE SKILLS

HTML and CSS are the most fundamental programming languages of the web. Now you've mastered them you can start building your own web pages. Knowing HTML and CSS is a great first step in a career in web design. Rather than using templates, you can create your own unique layouts – a fantastic skill. Mission accomplished!

CREATE A PASSWORD

- **LEARN TO USE HYPERLINKS TO CONNECT WEB PAGES**

- **LEARN WHAT JAVASCRIPT IS AND HOW IT WORKS**

- **WRITE PROGRAMS IN JAVASCRIPT THAT RUN IN YOUR WEB BROWSER**

- **PROTECT A WEB PAGE BY USING JAVASCRIPT TO CREATE A PASSWORD**

Dear Coder,

I'm Dr Ruby Day, the scientist on the expedition with Professor Bairstone. We were hoping to discover dinosaur fossils. Instead we've found the stolen Monk Diamond!

I want to tell you about a strange event. Yesterday we were examining the cave where we found the diamond. I heard a rumbling noise and Ernest started barking frantically. We looked up and saw a massive boulder rolling over the edge of the cliff above the cave! We jumped out of the way just in time, as the boulder landed exactly where we had been standing. In the commotion, Professor Bairstone tripped and sprained his ankle.

Professor Bairstone and I both agree the timing of the boulder is very suspicious. It seems too much of a coincidence for it to have happened just after we discovered a valuable stolen diamond. Professor Bairstone is convinced that the thieves have found out about our expedition and are trying to scare us off. He thinks the boulder is exactly the kind of dirty trick that the Bond Brothers, the main suspects in the Monk Diamond heist, would try.

We would leave the mountains now to take the diamond to safety, but unfortunately Professor Bairstone's sprained ankle means he can't make the treacherous descent just yet. While we are stuck in the mountains, I think the news about the discovery of the diamond needs to remain top secret. I am worried that the web page you built for Professor Bairstone could be accessed by the Bond Brothers and our safety compromised. Please could you add a password to the web page so that for now only Professor Bairstone and I can view the page? Use **Ernest300** as the password.

Thank you for all your help and hard work.

Very best wishes from the dangerous mountains,
Dr Ruby Day

PS Prof. B. has asked me to send you this entry from the Explorer's Encyclopedia.

The Bond Brothers

From the Explorer's Encyclopedia, the guide to every adventure

This entry is about the Bond Brothers. For more information about jewel robberies, see Jewel Thefts.

The **Bond Brothers** are a top secret international gang of jewel thieves. According to Interpol, over the last fifteen years they have stolen gems worth a total of more than £500 million.

The gang's tactics are similar to those used by the famous gang the Pink Panthers.

WANTED

FOR THE THEFT OF THE MONK DIAMOND
THE BOND BROTHERS

LIGHT FINGERS   **GEMMA THE GEM**   **TONY TWINKLES**

REWARD OF £1 MILLION

FOR INFORMATION LEADING TO THE RECOVERY OF THE MONK DIAMOND OR ARREST OF THE GANG

The Bond Brothers typically target exclusive jewellery houses and boutiques all over the world. Their raids are exceptionally well-planned, with the targets scoped out weeks in advance.

The Bond Brothers' tactics have included driving 4x4s through jewellery house windows and drilling through basements of boutiques to access valuables kept in vaults. Members of the gang have disguised themselves as workmen to confuse staff and then smashed open display cases.

Although the police were unable to prove it, most people think that the Bond Brothers are responsible for the unsolved theft of the Monk Diamond from the House of Volkov jewellery house in Moscow. Two members of the gang (a man and a woman) pretended to be looking for an engagement ring. While the woman distracted the staff, the man smashed open the Monk Diamond's display case with a pickaxe. The two then fled in a getaway car, which was posing as a taxi outside.

All the CCTV in and around the House of Volkov had been disabled for the hour in which the crime took place. Interpol therefore believes that one of the gang is also skilled in cyber-crime.

USING HYPERLINKS

In the Mission Brief Dr Day asked you to create a password. The password will stop the Bond Brothers finding out about the discovery of the Monk Diamond. In this mission you are going to learn how to make the password.

We have to use a new programming language called JavaScript to make the password. But before we can get started on coding the password, you first need to learn how to use HTML to link two web pages together. We need to be able to link the web page that asks the user to enter the password to the web page you built for Professor Bairstone.

Hyperlinks (or links, as they are normally known) are found on most web pages and are essential for creating the groups of web pages we call websites. A hyperlink can be a word, number, phrase or image that you click on. When you click on the link, your web browser takes you to either a different place in your current web page, or a completely new web page.

The anchor tag: <a> and </a>

Hyperlinks are made using a HTML tag called the anchor <a> tag. The opening tag is <a> and the closing tag is </a>. Inside the opening <a> tag you have to include an href attribute. The href attribute contains the URL (or web address) your browser needs to link to the new web page. Let's take a look:

Anchor tag **href attribute** **URL** **Hyperlink text**

```
<a href="https://www.monkdiamonddiscovery.com">Diamond Discovery</a>
```

We've set the value of our href attribute to the URL for the Monk Diamond Discovery page. We've done this in exactly the same way as we set the values of all the attributes in Mission 1: by using the equals sign (=) and double quotes (" ") to enclose the URL. The text between the opening and closing <a> tags becomes your link. When you click on this text you will be taken to the Monk Diamond page.

2

CODE SKILLS ► CREATING A HYPERLINK

Hyperlinks are an important skill to master when building websites as they let the user easily access pieces of content. Let's create a web page with a hyperlink.

1. Open up your text-editing program. Create a new HTML file called **links.html**. Type this code into your new file:

```
<!DOCTYPE html>
<html>
<head>
   <title>Links</title>
</head>
<body>
</body>
</html>
```

2. Let's make our hyperlink. Add an anchor <a> tag with an empty href attribute to the <body> of your page. Your code will look like this:

```
<body>
   <a href=" "></a>
</body>
```

3. Choose a word or phrase to be the text for your hyperlink on your web page. Put it between your opening and closing <a> tags. Your code will look like this:

```
<body>
   <a href=" ">Click here</a>
</body>
```

4. Now choose the URL you want your hyperlink to connect to. Set it as the value of your href attribute. Your code will look like this:

```
<body>
   <a href="https://www.google.co.uk">
      Click here</a>
</body>
```

5. Save your HTML file and open it in your web browser. You will see the text between your <a> tags displayed on-screen. When you click the hyperlink text your web browser will link to your URL.

Try clicking your new link!

Linking between web pages

To protect the information about the Monk Diamond, we first need to make a new web page. This new web page will be the first page that the user sees. If the user gets the password correct they will be sent to the Monk Diamond web page. If they get the password wrong, nothing will happen. By linking our pages together, we create a website.

We need to use a hyperlink to connect our two pages. If your web pages are saved in the same place on your computer, you don't need to provide your web browser with the URL – you can just use the file name as the URL. So if we make sure we have both HTML files saved in our **Coding** folder, we can use code like this:

File name

```
<a href="filename.html">Web page name<a/>
```

When we create our new password web page and save the HTML file in our **Coding** folder, we can link the new web page to the web page we built for Professor Bairstone in Mission 1 really easily. All we need to do is use the <a> tag and href attribute on each of our pages, like this:

Page 1: password.html

```
<!DOCTYPE html>
<html>
<head>
    <title>Password</title>
</head>
                    File name
<body>
    <a href="monkdiamonddiscovery.html">
    Click here to visit the Monk
    Diamond web page</a>
</body>
</html>
```

Page 2: monkdiamonddiscovery.html

```
<!DOCTYPE html>
<html>
<head>
    <title>The Monk Diamond</title>
</head>
                    File name
<body>
    <a href="password.html">
    Click here to log out</a>
</body>
</html>
```

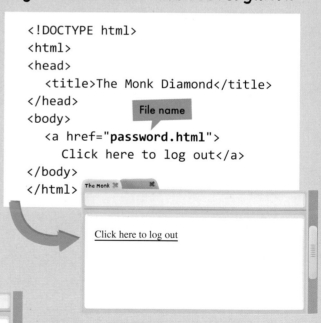

Click here to log out

Click here to visit the Monk Diamond web page

Clicking on the link in our password page takes us to our Monk Diamond web page. And clicking on the link in the Monk Diamond page takes us back to our password page.

CODE SKILLS ► LINKING BETWEEN WEB PAGES

Let's learn how to use hyperlinks to link together two web pages and build a very simple website.

1. Open up your text-editing program. Create a new HTML file called **page1.html**. Make sure it is saved in your **Coding** folder. Type this code into your new file:

```
<!DOCTYPE html>
<html>
<head>
   <title>Page 1</title>
</head>
<body>
</body>
</html>
```

2. Create a second HTML file called **page2.html**. Make sure it is saved in your **Coding** folder. Then copy and paste your code from **page1.html** into your new file. Modify the code so that it looks like this:

```
<!DOCTYPE html>
<html>
<head>
   <title>Page 2</title>
</head>
<body>
</body>
</html>
```

3. Now create a hyperlink that connects your first page to your second page. On your first page, add the <a> tag with an href attribute. Set the value of the href to the file name of your second page. Then add some text between the opening and closing <a> tags to make your hyperlink, like this:

```
<body>
   <a href="page2.html">Page 2</a>
</body>
```

4. Now open your second page. Create a hyperlink that takes you back to your first page. Your code will look like this:

```
<body>
   <a href="page1.html">Back to Page 1</a>
</body>
```

Save your files and open them in your browser. You will be able to link between the two pages.

Now to make the password!

CODING WITH JAVASCRIPT

Hyperlinks are an important first step in creating a web page that responds to the user. But if we want to code a page that is really interactive and changes according to what the user does, we need to use a new programming language called JavaScript with our HTML.

JavaScript is the most popular programming language in the world. It transforms a HTML and CSS web page by making it interactive. We need JavaScript to do all sorts of useful things, such as making buttons and alerts and storing information. In this mission we are going to learn how we can

use JavaScript with HTML to create a password, so that the information about the Monk Diamond is kept safe from the cyber-criminal in the Bond Brothers gang.

We saw in Mission 1 how HTML documents are made up of different elements and that you use attributes to change those elements. JavaScript also has its own syntax, or set of rules, for writing code. JavaScript syntax is made up of pieces of code called statements, variables, operators and functions. Let's learn about them and see how we can use them to build the password.

Adding JavaScript to your HTML page

Before you can start writing JavaScript you need to tell your browser that you are switching from HTML to JavaScript. You do this by using the <script> tag. If you don't put your JavaScript code between the opening and closing <script> tags your code won't run. You can have as many <script> tags as you want in your HTML document and you can put them inside either the <head> or <body> on your page.

```
<!DOCTYPE html>
<html>
<head>
    <title>Password</title>
</head>
<body>
    <script>          ← Script tag
    </script>
</body>
</html>
```

Here the <script> tag is inside the <body> of our page. Sometimes we call this a <script> block.

Statements

When we write an instruction for our browser in JavaScript, we call this writing a statement. JavaScript programs normally contain many statements. A statement usually starts with a keyword that tells you what action it will perform. It always ends with a semi-colon (;). Your browser runs one statement after another in the order they are written. Let's look at some JavaScript statements. When we save this code and run it in our browser, this happens:

```
<!DOCTYPE html>
<html>
<head>
  <title>Password</title>
</head>
<body>
  <script>
    alert("We need a password urgently!");
    alert("Use the password Ernest300");
  </script>
</body>
</html>
```

Semi-colon

Statements

The two statements between the opening and closing <script> tags have run one after another, popping up two alert boxes with different messages inside. An alert is a piece of JavaScript called a function, and it's built in to your web browser. We'll learn more about it later in the mission.

JavaScript is case sensitive, so it's important to make sure you have used the correct capital letters. If you have to choose a name for a piece of JavaScript, you can't leave spaces between words. A good way to write two words is to use **camelCase**.

CODE WORDS

camelCase is the practice of joining two words together to form one word. The first word starts with a lower-case letter and the second word begins with an upper-case letter, but there is no space between them, just like the humps of a camel. An example of camelCase is sayHello.

VARIABLES

These are important!

Variables are an important part of JavaScript. They are a way to store information in your web browser for a short period of time. You can then use the stored data to build programs that make your web page interactive. Without variables your browser has no way of remembering information.

So when we use JavaScript to code a program that will check a password, we need to use a variable to store the data for the correct password. Without a variable our browser won't be able to check if the user has entered a correct password.

Variables store data in the form of words or numbers. You have to code variables in a certain way. You always have to tell your browser you are creating a variable. This is called defining a variable. Let's have a look at how we create a variable that will store Ernest's name:

Ernest is a very good name!

```
var dogName = "Ernest";
```

Variable keyword   Variable name   Value

Variables are always written in the same way. Every piece of JavaScript tells your browser a different piece of information, and will be important when you build a program.

A variable needs:

- **A keyword**
  To define a variable you have to use the variable (var) keyword. It tells your browser you are creating a variable.

- **A variable name**
  The next part of a variable is the variable name. You can give your variable any name you like. The only rule with variable names is that they can't have spaces (so use camelCase instead) and can't begin with a number.

- **A value**
  You then have to give your variable a value using the equals sign (=). Doing this is called assigning a value. If the value of your variable is text, you have to put the value in double quotes (" "). You can include spaces in your values. After the value you have to include a semi-colon (;).

Operators

Operators are another key part of JavaScript. They are a way of changing the value of a variable. Different kinds of operators do different things to the information in your variable.

Assignment operators

Can you spot the use of camelCase?

Assignment operators allow you to create and set the values of your variables.

Equals (=): you use the equals sign (=) to give your variable a value. You can use it to set variables to both numbers and words. If your variable is a number, it doesn't have to be in double quotes (" "). Here's an example where the value is set to a number:

```
var teamMembers = 3;
```

Assignment operator

And here's an example where the value is set to words and needs double quotes (" "):

```
var expeditionLeader = "Professor Bairstone";
```

Arithmetic operators

Arithmetic operators are a way of using maths calculations to change the values of your variables. They are a useful way of creating a numerical value for a variable.

Addition (+): you use the addition operator (+) to add together numbers to create a value. Here the value of our campRations variable will be set to 3.

```
var campRations = 2 + 1;
```

Addition operator

Subtraction operator

Subtraction (−): you use the subtraction operator (−) to subtract numbers to create a value. Here the value of our dogBiscuits variable will be set to 1.

```
var dogBiscuits = 5 - 4;
```

Always make sure you use a semi-colon at the end of the variable.

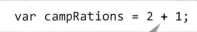

Don't forget to put text values in double quotes.

Variables and operators are important parts of the JavaScript programming language. Let's code some simple JavaScript programs using them.

1. Before we can write any JavaScript we need to create a HTML file with a `<script>` tag in the `<body>`. Open up your text-editing program. Create a new HTML file called **variables.html**. Type this code into your new file:

```
<!DOCTYPE html>
<html>
<head>
    <title>Variables</title>
</head>
<body>
    <script>
    </script>
</body>
</html>
```

2. Now try writing some JavaScript. Create a variable between the opening and closing `<script>` tags. Give your variable a name and then use the assignment operator (=) to set the value of your variable. Let's try with a number, like this:

```
<script>
    var diamondCarats = 300;
</script>
```

Don't forget JavaScript is case sensitive, so make sure you keep the cases the same in your code block. Also remember the semi-colon (;) at the end. If you save your HTML file and open it in your browser, nothing will happen – but don't worry. You have stored 300 in your diamondCarats variable.

3. Let's use the alert function to check that your variable has been stored in your browser. Underneath your variable type this code:

```
<script>
    var diamondCarats = 300;
    alert(diamondCarats);
</script>
```

What we're doing is asking our browser to run the built-in alert function. Whatever value is in our diamondCarats variable will be displayed in an alert.

Check that pop-ups haven't been disabled in your browser. Search online for how to disable the pop-up blocker in the browser you are using.

Save your HTML file and refresh your page. An alert will pop up and you will see the value of your diamondCarats variable displayed on-screen. Click OK and your alert will vanish. Refresh your page and the alert will reload.

4. Now let's code a new variable, using the addition operator (+), to find the total number of people and dogs in Professor Bairstone's team. Let's call our variable teamMembers and set an alert to show the value of our variable. Modify the <script> block so that it looks like this:

```
<script>
   var teamMembers = 2 + 1;
   alert(teamMembers);
</script>
```

Save your file and refresh your page. Your alert will be the value of your teamMembers variable. Click OK.

5. Finally, let's try creating a variable using the assignment operator (=) to store text in our variable. Don't forget that you need double quote marks (" ") around the text. Set an alert to show the value of your variable. Modify the code in your file so that it looks like this:

```
<script>
   var jewelThieves = "The Bond Brothers";
   alert(jewelThieves);
</script>
```

 When you save your file and refresh your page, you will see your text displayed in an alert.

Well done! You've just written your first JavaScript programs!

COMPARISON OPERATORS

As well as assigning values or performing maths calculations, operators can be used to compare the values of variables. Being able to compare values allows us to make our web pages more interactive. Using comparison operators we can write code that does different things depending on the values of our variables. Here are some of the different comparison operators you can use:

These operators can be used in JavaScript statements to ask questions about our variables. Then we can write code that makes different things happen depending on the answer to the question. Instructions for our browser that use comparison operators are called if statements and else statements. These types of statement are called conditionals, because they depend on the value, or condition, of the variable.

Operator	Meaning
==	Equal to
!=	Not equal to
>	Greater than
<	Less than
>=	Greater than or equal to
<=	Less than or equal to

IF STATEMENTS

If statements are a way of telling our browser to perform an instruction only if the condition of our variable is true. If the condition of our variable is false, our browser won't perform the instruction in the code.

We have to structure if statements in a certain way. We start them with the statement keyword (if). Then we open a pair of brackets and put the rule for our if statement inside them. Then we open a pair of curly braces ({ }). Inside them we put the instruction we want to happen only when our if statement is true.

Let's have a look at an example where we've used the equal to operator (==) to create an if statement. Here the value of our variable is set to Dr Day using the assignment operator (=). We then create an if statement by asking our browser to check if the value in our variable is equal to (==) Dr Day. Then we ask our browser to pop up an alert if our condition is true.

Equal to operator

Curly brace

If statement

Alert

```
<script>
    var person = "Dr Day";
    if(person == "Dr Day") {
        alert("Hello Dr Day!");
    }
</script>
```

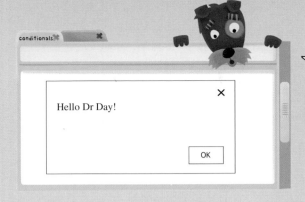

> We've used an if statement to code a program that will say hello to Dr Day!

Now, if we change the value of our variable to a value that isn't equal to Dr Day, nothing will happen. This is because the if statement is false. Our browser won't run the code inside the curly braces and no alert will pop up.

```
<script>
  var person = "Ernest";
  if(person == "Dr Day") {
      alert("Hello Dr Day!");
  }
</script>
```

You can use the other comparison operators in that table to check all sorts of different things. You can see if things are not equal to (!=), or you can use the greater than (>) and less than (<) operators to check if a number is bigger or smaller than another number. Let's have a look at using the greater than operator (>) to create an if statement.

Greater than operator

```
<script>
  var diamondCarats = 300;
  if(diamondCarats > 299) {
      alert("Valuable Diamond Alert!");
  }
</script>
```

Here the value of our variable is set to 300. We create an if statement by asking our browser to check if the value in our variable is greater than (>) 299. Then we ask our browser to pop up an alert if our condition is true. The Monk Diamond is 300 carats, so the alert will pop up.

> Notice how the closing curly brace lines up with the keyword.

Using if statements in your JavaScript code means you can build more complex programs that change according to the value in a variable. Let's build a program that uses an if statement.

1. Open up your text-editing program. Create a new HTML file called **ifstatements.html**. Type this code into your new file:

```
<!DOCTYPE html>
<html>
<head>
    <title>Conditionals</title>
</head>
<body>
    <script>
    </script>
</body>
```

2. Create an if statement using the equal to operator (==). Make an alert pop up if the condition of a variable is true. First, create a variable called dogName between your `<script>` tags. Then create your if statement and alert. Don't forget to put the instruction for the if statement in brackets and the instruction for your alert in curly braces ({ }). Your code will look like this:

```
<script>
  var dogName = "Ernest";
  if(dogName == "Ernest") {
    alert("You discovered the Monk Diamond!");
  }
</script>
```

3. Save your HTML file and open it in your browser. An alert will pop up.

I certainly did discover that diamond! It wasn't such a clever hiding place after all.

4. In the value of your variable try changing Ernest to your own name, so the condition of the if statement is false. Save your file and refresh your page. The alert will not pop up.

ELSE STATEMENTS

Else statements are used with if statements to make web pages even more interactive. You use an else statement after an if statement to change which block of code is run by your browser. If the condition of your if statement is false, your browser will run the alternative else statement.

Else statements are written in exactly the same way as if statements – you just have to use the else keyword instead. You put the code you want to run inside curly braces ({ }). Let's take a look at an example of an if statement and an else statement working together:

```
<script>
  var name = "Tony Twinkles";
  if(name == "Dr Day") {
    alert("Access Granted!");
  }
  else {
    alert("Access Denied!");
  }
</script>
```

Else statement

If we run this code in our browser an alert will pop up. The value in our variable is the name of one of the Bond Brothers and not equal to (==) Dr Day. Because the condition of the if statement was false, our browser ran the else statement. But if the value of our variable had been equal to (==) Dr Day and the condition of our if statement had been true, the else statement would not have run. The if statement would have run instead, and the "Access Granted" alert would have popped up.

That's a clever way to stop the Bond Brothers!

Hmph! How am I going to find out if they have the jewel?

Now we should learn how to use an else statement with an if statement in a block of JavaScript code. Let's try coding a program that uses both types of conditional statement.

1. Open up your text-editing program. Create a new HTML file called **elsestatements.html**. Then copy and paste your code from **ifstatements.html** into your new file. Modify the code so that it looks like this:

```
<!DOCTYPE html>
<html>
<head>
    <title>Conditionals</title>
</head>
<body>
    <script>
    </script>
</body>
```

2. Create a new if statement in your `<script>` block using the less than or equal to operator (`<=`) . Make the condition of your if statement false. Your code will look like this:

```
<script>
    var diamondValue = 10;
    if(diamondValue <= 9.9) {
        alert("Value: Under £10 million!");
    }
</script>
```

3. Now add an else statement after your if statement. This statement will run if the condition of the if statement is false. Your code will look like this:

```
<script>
    var diamondValue = 10;
    if(diamondValue <= 9.9) {
        alert("Value: Under £10 million!");
    }
    else {
        alert("Value: Over £10 million!");
    }
</script>
```

4. Save your HTML file and open it in your browser. Your else statement will run and an alert will pop up.

WRITING JAVASCRIPT

- JavaScript always has to be written inside the `<script>` tag, so that your browser knows you are switching from HTML to a new programming language. You can put `<script>` tags in the `<head>` or `<body>` of your page.

- Just like HTML and CSS, JavaScript is written in a special way and has its own syntax. It is a case-sensitive language. You should leave spaces between pieces of code to make them easier to read.

- Each instruction you give your browser in JavaScript is called a statement. Statements have to end in a semi-colon (;). Curly braces ({ }) are used to group statements together into a block of code to be run in one go by your browser.

- Statements normally start with a keyword that tells you the action the statement will perform.

- You can store information in your browser using variables. Variables have a name and a value, which can be either text or numbers. If the value is text it has to be in double quotes (" "). If your variable name has two words, write it using camelCase.

- To change or set the values of your variables you can use assignment operators, arithmetic operators and comparison operators.

- If statements and else statements are known as conditional statements. Using conditional statements allows us to make our code do different things depending on the value of a variable.

> Using JavaScript helps us make interactive web pages that respond to the user.

FUNCTIONS

Another important part of JavaScript coding is learning how to create and use functions. You create a function by grouping together JavaScript statements. The statements grouped in the function work together to perform a particular action. The function won't run until you tell your browser to run it. This is known as calling a function. Let's take a look at how you create a function that will pop up an alert and then call it:

Function name

Function keyword

```
<script>
    function sayPassword() {
        alert("Password!");
    }
    sayPassword();
</script>
```

Statement

Function call

Function ✖ ✖

Password!

×

OK

Functions always have to be written in the same way. Each part is an important instruction for your browser.

A function needs:

- **The function keyword**
  To define and create a function you have to use the function keyword.

- **A function name**
  Then you need to give your function a name. The name should be short and explain the action the function performs. The name always ends with a pair of brackets.

- **Curly braces**
  After the function name you have to open a pair of curly braces ({ }). All the statements you want to group together in the function have to go inside the curly braces.

- **Statements**
  Statements form the body of your function. You can use as many statements as you want and the block of code will run in your browser whenever you call the function.

- **A function call**
  To call our function and run the block of code, you have to type the name of the function (including the brackets) followed by a semi-colon. After you have defined your function, you can call your function anywhere in your <script> block.

Built-in functions

As well as grouping together statements to create your own functions, you can also use functions that are built into your browser. A built-in function is an action your browser knows how to perform without you having to write any code. A programmer has already done the hard work for you. All you have to do is give your browser the name of the built-in function and the information it needs to run.

JavaScript has many built-in functions. You've already been using one in this mission: the alert function. To use the alert function, all you do is type "alert" and your browser pops up the alert box. Built-in functions save you time and let you do more complex things when you are programming.

Functions and arguments

To make a function perform a task, you sometimes have to give it a piece of information so it can run. When we put information inside a function, we say that we have passed our function an argument. You have been passing an argument to a function every time you have used the alert function. Let's take a look at what an argument looks like:

Argument

Function

```
alert("Access Denied!");
```

The information in brackets after the name of the function is our argument. Our browser needs the argument to know what text to display in the alert box. Without the argument, the alert function wouldn't work properly.

Arguments can be in the form of text, numbers or variables. If you are passing your function a piece of text to use as an argument, it needs to be in double quotes (" "). If you are passing it the name of a variable, you just use the variable name without quotes, like this:

```
var bondBrothers = "Dangerous jewel thieves!";
alert(bondBrothers);
```

Variable passed as argument

You can pass arguments to any kind of function. You might have wondered why function names and function calls always end with a pair of brackets. It's so you can pass the function an argument. Turn over to see how to do it.

```
<script>
  function sayHello(name) {
    alert("Hello " + name);
  }
  sayHello("Dr Day!");
</script>
```

Argument added to function

Function call

Hello Dr Day!

OK

In this piece of code we have created a function that will pop up an alert. We do this by adding an argument to our function. This kind of argument is called a parameter. We then code an alert which tells our browser to pop up some text plus the argument. We then tell the browser the name to insert in the alert by putting it in the function call.

The return statement

So far we have been giving our functions pieces of information in arguments. We can also make our functions give us pieces of information back as values. When a function gives back a piece of information, we say it has returned the information. To make a function return a piece of information, we have to use a return statement inside the function. The value in the return statement can be text, numbers or a variable, and it becomes the value of the function. Let's take a look at how we can use a return statement to give us a piece of text:

```
<script>
  function getName() {
    return "Dr Day";
  }
  var scientist = getName();
  alert(scientist);
</script>
```

Function name

Return statement

Value to return

Dr Day

OK

Functions will often perform an action and return the result to the rest of your code.

In this example we've created a function called getName. We want our function to give us Dr Day's name as a value, so we've used a return statement and set her name as the value. We've then stored the function name as the variable value. When the alert pops up, it will pop up with the value of the return.

► FUNCTIONS AND ARGUMENTS

Let's have a go at grouping together statements and creating a function. We should also try out the return statement as it will be very useful when we create our password for Dr Day.

1. Open up your text-editing program. Create a new HTML file called **functions.html**. Type this code into your new file:

```
<!DOCTYPE html>
<html>
<head>
   <title>Functions</title>
</head>
<body>
   <script>
   </script>
</body>
</html>
```

2. Inside your `<script>` block create a function called checkAccess that will pop up an alert when you call it. Your code will look like this:

```
<script>
   function checkAccess() {
      alert("Restricted access!");
   }
   checkAccess();
</script>
```

3. Save your HTML file and open it in your browser. An alert will pop up.

4. Now change your checkAccess function so that it contains a return statement. Store the name of your function in a variable. Then make an alert pop up to show the value of your variable:

```
<script>
   function checkAccess() {
      return "Expedition team only!";
   }
   var webPage = checkAccess();
   alert(webPage);
</script>
```

 Save and refresh your page. A new alert will pop up.

MAKING JAVASCRIPT WORK WITH HTML

We've seen throughout this mission how you can add JavaScript to your HTML web page by writing it inside the <script> tag. But now we need to learn how to make our JavaScript code run when the user clicks on a HTML element. If we want something to happen when the user clicks on a piece of text or an image on our page, we have to add JavaScript to our HTML tags. Luckily there's an attribute that lets us do this.

Attributes! You know all about them from Mission 1.

The onclick attribute

It's really easy to make a piece of JavaScript run when the user clicks on a HTML element on your page. All you need to do is include the onclick attribute (or the "onclick") in the HTML tag you want to make interactive. Then when the user clicks on the HTML element in their browser, the JavaScript code will run.

The onclick attribute is just like all the other attributes we've used in the missions so far. You add the attribute to the opening tag of the HTML element you want the user to click on. You then set the value of the onclick to the piece of JavaScript you want to run, using the equals sign (=) and double quotes (" "). Don't forget the semi-colon (;). You can put any JavaScript you want inside an onclick. Let's take a look:

```
<!DOCTYPE html>
<html>
<head>
   <title>Diamond Colour</title>
</head>                    Onclick attribute        Value set to
<body>                                             JavaScript
   <p onclick="alert('Green');">
      Click here to find out the colour of the Monk Diamond
   </p>
</body>
</html>
```

When the user clicks on the text between the opening and closing <p> tags, the JavaScript function in our onclick runs. An alert will pop up.

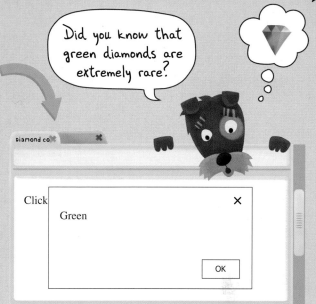

Did you notice?

We used single quotes (' ') around the argument we passed to our alert function. This is because we had already used double quotes to set the value of the onclick attribute. Always use single quotes inside double quotes, or your code won't run.

Using true and false with the return statement

You can also use your onclick attribute to stop your browser following an instruction in a piece of code. To do this you use a return statement in your onclick, and set its value to "false".

Return is a **reserved word** in JavaScript. If you use a return statement and set it to the value "true", your browser will keep running the code. But if you use "false" as a value in your return statement, your browser will stop running the code immediately.

CODE WORDS

RESERVED WORDS are words that cannot be used as function or variable names. This is because they are special commands that your browser understands. You don't need to put reserved words in double quotes (" ").

The onclick attribute and hyperlinks

We can create a very useful piece of JavaScript with the onclick attribute and the value "false". You can use the onclick and the return statement to stop a hyperlink from working when a user clicks on it. This will be very useful when we code our password later in the mission. If the user gets the password wrong, they won't be taken to the Monk Diamond web page.

To do this, you first create your hyperlink in exactly the same way as we did at the start of the mission, using the anchor <a> tag and the href attribute, like this:

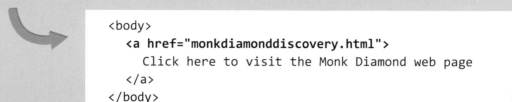

```
<body>
   <a href="monkdiamonddiscovery.html">
      Click here to visit the Monk Diamond web page
   </a>
</body>
```

Then you add the onclick attribute and the return statement. Set the value of the return statement to "false", like this:

Return statement   False value

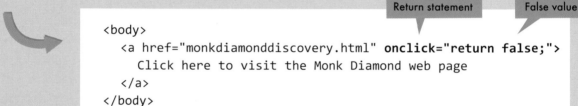

```
<body>
   <a href="monkdiamonddiscovery.html" onclick="return false;">
      Click here to visit the Monk Diamond web page
   </a>
</body>
```

Using "false" as the value of our onclick means that nothing will happen when the user clicks on the link.

This will help keep our web page hidden!

2

CODE SKILLS ► MAKING HTML CODE RUN JAVASCRIPT

Practise using the HTML onclick attribute to run a piece of JavaScript code. Knowing how to do this will mean you can make HTML elements respond to the user.

1. Open up your text-editing program. Create a new HTML file called **onclick.html**. Type this code into your new file:

```
<!DOCTYPE html>
<html>
<head>
    <title>Onclick</title>
</head>
<body>
</body>
</html>
```

2. In your <body> create a hyperlink that will take your user to Google. Use the anchor <a> tag and href attribute. Set the value to the Google URL. Your code will look like this:

```
<body>
    <a href="https://www.google.com">
    Google
    </a>
</body>
```

3. Now add your onclick attribute to your opening <a> tag. Set the value of your onclick to a JavaScript alert. Remember to use single quotes (' ') for the alert argument. Your code will look like this:

```
<a href="https://www.google.com" onclick="alert('Redirecting to Google');">
    Google
</a>
```

4. Save your HTML file and open it in your browser. When you click on the link an alert will pop up. When you click OK, you will be taken to Google.

5. Now stop your hyperlink from taking you to Google. Use a return statement in your onclick like this:

```
<a href="https://www.google.com" onclick="return false;">
    Google
</a>
```

 Save your file and refresh your page. When you click on the link, your page won't connect to Google.

CREATING YOUR PASSWORD PAGE

Now you know how to use the onclick attribute to make your HTML elements interactive, we can start building our password web page for Dr Day.
Let's start with the basic HTML structure of our page:

```
<!DOCTYPE html>
<html>
<head>
   <title>Password</title>
<style>
   body {
      background-color: lightblue;
      padding: 30px;
   }
</style>
</head>
<body>
   <p style="font-size: 30pt;">THE MONK DIAMOND DISCOVERY</p>
   <p>Please enter the password to view this website.</p>
   <p>Password:</p>
   <a href="monkdiamonddiscovery.html">
      Click here to submit password and view website
   </a>
</body>
</html>
```

CSS class

Hyperlink

Don't forget the top secret password is **Ernest300**.

Here we've created a simple web page using HTML and CSS. We've included a hyperlink that links to our Monk Diamond Discovery web page. But there isn't anywhere on our page where the user can enter their password. We need to create a box so that the user can type it in.

Password

THE MONK DIAMOND DISCOVERY

Please enter the password to view this website.

Password:

Click here to submit password and view website

The input tag: <input/>

Websites often need you to type in information. It's how you log in to an online account, book cinema tickets or use a search engine. So asking your user to type in information is a common part of coding. It's called asking for user input.

There are lots of tags you can use to ask for user input, but the one you will use the most is the <input/> tag. It's great for creating boxes on your page so your user can enter data. It's a self-closing tag and you include two attributes inside it: the id attribute and the type attribute. As you already know, you set the value of these attributes using the equals sign (=) and double quotes (" "). Let's take a look at how we would use the <input/> tag on our page:

```
<body>
  <p style="font-size: 30pt;">THE MONK DIAMOND DISCOVERY</p>
  <p>Please enter the password to view this website.</p>
  <p>Password:<input id="passwordBox" type="text"/></p>
  <a href="monkdiamonddiscovery.html">
    Click here to submit password and view website
  </a>
</body>
```

Type attribute

Id attribute

Using the <input/> tag with these two attributes creates a box that we can type our password into.

You use the id attribute to give your <input/> tag a unique name. You have to choose the name of your id attribute. Make sure it's easy to remember. Here we've set the value of the id attribute to passwordBox.

Doing this allows us to use the value inside the <input/> tag in our JavaScript. We use the id attribute to tell our browser exactly which piece of data we want it to use. Without the id attribute your browser will not be able to find the password and check if the password is correct.

THE MONK DIAMOND DISCOVERY

Please enter the password to view this website.

Password: Ernest300

Click here to submit password and view website

Look, you can enter the password!

The type attribute

There are lots of different kinds of `<input/>` tags, so you need to use the type attribute to tell your browser exactly what sort of `<input/>` tag you need. You have to choose from defined values for your type attribute. Here are some of the common type attributes you can use inside your `<input/>` tag:

Attribute value	What does it do?
text	Creates a box for entering text
password	Creates a box for entering a password
button	Creates a clickable button (with JavaScript)
checkbox	Creates a box the user can tick or untick

You may have noticed on the previous page that when we set the type attribute to text, the text for the password was displayed in the box. That isn't very secure! What happens if the Bond Brothers are near by when Dr Day types in the password?

If we want to keep our password secret we can change the value of our type attribute to password. This will hide what the user types by changing the text to dots. Let's take a look:

```
<body>
   <p style="font-size: 30pt;">THE MONK DIAMOND DISCOVERY</p>
   <p>Please enter the password to view this website.</p>
   <p>Password:<input id="passwordBox" type="password"/></p>
   <a href="monkdiamonddiscovery.html">
      Click here to submit password and view website
   </a>
</body>
```

Password value

That's a much better way of keeping the password secret!

THE MONK DIAMOND DISCOVERY

Please enter the password to view this website.

Password: •••••••••

Click here to submit password and view website

Using JavaScript to check the password

Now we've built the basic HTML structure of our page, we need to write some JavaScript that will check if the password the user enters is correct. If they enter the password Ernest300 they will be taken to the Monk Diamond Discovery page. If they enter an incorrect password an alert will pop up telling them they have got the password wrong.

The first thing we need to do is create a function that will contain all the code we need to check our password. Let's create the function inside our <head>. You can put JavaScript anywhere in a HTML web page, and having it in our <head> in this example makes our code easier to understand. Don't forget to put your JavaScript inside the <script> tag, like this:

```
<script>
  function checkPassword() {
  }
</script>
```
Function

We then need to create variables that store the value of our password, so that our function can check if the user has got it correct. Let's look at the two variables we need:

```
<script>
  function checkPassword() {
    var password = document.getElementById("passwordBox");
    var passwordEntered = password.value;
  }
</script>
```
Variable 1
Variable 2
getElementById
Id attribute

In our first variable we are using a new built-in function called getElementById. You will learn all about this function and use it more in Mission 3. It is a handy function that finds the HTML element with the specified id attribute. The id attribute we have selected here is for our <input/> tag. So the value of our variable will be whatever data the user has typed into the password box.

We then create a second variable to store the data that the user has typed into the password box. We create this value by typing the name of our first variable followed by a dot (.) then the value keyword. We do this so we can write an if statement using the value of this variable.

We now need to create an if statement. If the condition of our second variable is true and our password text is equal to (==) Ernest300, the hyperlink will work. If the condition of our variable is false and the password text is not equal to Ernest300, the link won't work and an alert will pop up. We don't need to use an else statement because the return statement will halt the function.

Turn the page to see what that code looks like!

Our complete `<script>` block for our password with the new if statement looks like this:

```
<script>
  function checkPassword() {
    var password = document.getElementById("passwordBox");
    var passwordText = password.value;
    if(passwordText == "Ernest300") {
      return true;
    }
    alert("Access denied! Incorrect password!");
    return false;
  }
</script>
```

If statement → `if(passwordText == "Ernest300") {`

Alert → `alert("Access denied! Incorrect password!");`

Finally we have to make our JavaScript work with our HTML elements. We need to look at the code in the `<body>` of our page now. We want to call the checkPassword function when someone clicks on the hyperlink in our page. So we need to add an onclick attribute to our opening `<a>` tag, like this:

```
<body>
  <p style="font-size: 30pt;">THE MONK DIAMOND DISCOVERY</p>
  <p>Please enter the password to view this website.</p>
  <p>Password:<input id="passwordBox" type="password"/></p>
  <a href="monkdiamonddiscovery.html" onclick="return checkPassword();">
    Click here to submit password and view website
  </a>
</body>
```

Function call → `onclick="return checkPassword();"`

Incorrect password

Correct password

90

DO IT YOURSELF TASK
CREATE A PASSWORD

It's time to have a go at using all the JavaScript Code Skills you've learnt in this mission to create a new web page that asks the user to enter a password. This web page will protect the web page you built in Mission 1. If the user gets the password right, they will be able to access the Monk Diamond Discovery web page. If they get it wrong, an alert will pop up telling them that access is denied.

The Monk Diamond Discovery Password Brief

When you build your new web page make sure you code these things using HTML and JavaScript:

- **A function** that will check your password when it is called.
- **Variables** that will store the value of the data the user enters into the password box.
- **An if statement** that will check if the password the user enters is correct.
- **An alert** that will pop up if an incorrect password is entered.
- **A text box** the user can enter data into.
- **A hyperlink** that connects this web page to the Monk Diamond Discovery web page.

Save your file in your **Coding** folder and call it **password.html**.

> Turn over to see the code you need for your password page.

```html
<!DOCTYPE html>
<html>
<head>
   <title>Password</title>
   <style>
     body {
        background-color: lightblue;
        padding: 30px;
     }
   </style>
   <script>
     function checkPassword() {
        var password = document.getElementById("passwordBox");
        var passwordText = password.value;
        if(passwordText == "Ernest300") {
           return true;
        }
        alert("Access denied! Incorrect password!");
        return false;
     }
   </script>
</head>
<body>
  <p style="font-size: 30pt;">THE MONK DIAMOND DISCOVERY</p>
  <p>Please enter the password to view this website.</p>
  <p>Password:<input id="passwordBox" type="password"/></p>
  <a href="monkdiamonddiscovery.html" onclick="return
     checkPassword();">
     Click here to submit password and view website
  </a>
</body>
</html>
```

The Bond Brothers won't beat us!

92

Password ✖ ✖

THE MONK DIAMOND DISCOVERY

Please enter the password to view this website.

Password: •••••••••

Click here to submit password and view website

Brilliant coding! This password page will keep the Monk Diamond safe. Don't forget you can use more CSS properties to change the look of the page.

FUTURE CODE SKILLS

JavaScript is a powerful and dynamic programming language, used by all modern web browsers. Knowing JavaScript allows you to create interactive and responsive web pages that allow a user to enter information. It's also great for building web-based apps.

Mission 3

BUILD AN APP

- **CREATE A BUTTON USING JAVASCRIPT**

- **PROGRAM YOUR WEB BROWSER USING THE DOCUMENT OBJECT MODEL (DOM) API**

- **LEARN TO MAKE YOUR WEB PAGE REMEMBER THINGS WITH THE LOCALSTORAGE API**

- **BUILD A TO-DO LIST APP**

Dear Coder,

You'll be pleased to hear that there are no more suspicious events to report. I think that the work you did for Dr Day has been a success and, unable to access our web page, the Bond Brothers have been thrown off our trail. Once again you impress me!

My injured ankle has now healed. We left the mountains yesterday and are currently on the Trans-Siberian Railway to Moscow. Our first class carriage is very luxurious and I've been emailing my old and dear friend, Mr Viktor Volkov of the House of Volkov. As you already know, the House of Volkov is where the Monk Diamond was so audaciously stolen from three years ago. It is one of the oldest and most respected jewellery houses in the world and Mr Volkov was devastated by the theft.

I have told Mr Volkov about our discovery. At first he couldn't believe it! But finally I convinced him and he wants us to return to Moscow with the diamond as quickly as possible. Already he is making plans for a special exhibition. He will invite the most important jewel collectors from all over the world and announce our discovery.

Mr Volkov needs help with planning the exhibition. As we're on the train, I was hoping once again you might be able to help. Is there any way you could build a to-do list app? We can use the app to keep track of all the different tasks we need to do between now and the opening of the exhibition. I can be quite absent-minded, so having the app would be really useful.

If we don't plan the exhibition properly (and with maximum security), I'm worried the Bond Brothers might try to steal back the diamond. I'm attaching some notes about what needs to be done before the opening of the exhibition and also an entry from the Explorer's Encyclopedia about the House of Volkov, which will help you build the app.

Warmest regards from my comfortable carriage,
Professor Harry Bairstone

The House of Volkov

From the Explorer's Encyclopedia, the guide to every adventure

THE EXPLORER'S ENCYCLOPEDIA
The Guide to Every Adventure

Volkov diamonds redirects here.

The **House of Volkov** is one of the world's oldest jewellery houses, famous for its high quality diamond jewellery. It also has a world-renowned private collection of gems.

The House of Volkov was founded in St Petersburg in the 1790s. It was founded by Vladimir Volkov, who became known as the Prince of Diamonds for his love of the most rare and valuable stones. The House of Volkov was appointed as the official

The Monk Diamond Special Exhibition
To-Do List

- Commission a state-of-the-art unbreakable glass display case
- Order a new velvet cushion for the diamond
- Hire private security
- Hire a bodyguard to protect Mr Volkov
- Invite guests
- Buy diamond-themed snacks and lemonade
- Buy dog biscuits for Ernest

jeweller of the Imperial Court, supplying the Russian nobility with beautiful jewellery in intricate designs.

Today the House of Volkov is located on one of the most exclusive streets in Moscow, near to St Basil's Cathedral. Volkov diamonds are still renowned for their quality and are some of the most expensive in the world.

Viktor Volkov, the current owner, bought the Monk Diamond for an undisclosed sum at auction. It was the centrepiece of the House of Volkov's private collection. It was displayed to the public in an antique glass case until it was stolen in a smash-and-grab robbery. The theft of the Monk Diamond remains unsolved. Since the robbery the House of Volkov has reported a sharp drop in sales and there are rumours that it might be sold. Mr Volkov said in a recent interview, "I would be devastated if the business, which has been in my family for generations, had to close."

The House of Volkov

Industry:	Jewellers
Founded:	1794
Founder:	Vladimir Volkov
Headquarters:	Moscow
Area served:	Worldwide

BUILDING A WEB-BASED APP

Planning the special exhibition for the Monk Diamond at the House of Volkov is going to be a big job for Professor Bairstone, Dr Day and Mr Volkov. In this mission you are going to help them by building an app that will run in your web browser. Professor Bairstone can use this app to create his to-do list. Once he's done a task, he can remove it from the list.

We're going to need to learn some new JavaScript functions to build our app. At the moment the web pages we've built don't change after your browser has drawn them on-screen. Professor Bairstone is going to want to add and remove items from his list, so our app needs to be more interactive. Let's have a look at what our app will look like:

Text box

Button for adding items to list

Items removed from list when clicked

Our app will have a text box that Professor Bairstone can type into. When he clicks on the button, the item will be added to the list. When he's completed a task, he can click on it and it will be removed. We can code all these things using the JavaScript you learnt in Mission 2 with some new programming tools.

Building a text box and button

Before we start learning new JavaScript code, let's build the basic structure of our app. We need a text box and a button. In Mission 2 you learnt how to use the `<input/>` tag and the type attribute. We're going to be using those skills again in this mission.

The `<input/>` tag allows you to create a HTML element on your page where your user can enter data. You use the type attribute to choose the kind of element your user can add data to. So to create a text box and a clickable button on our page, we will need the following code:

```
<input type="text"/>
<input type="button"/>
```

3

We also need to add some text inside the text box and button, so the user knows what action they perform. We do this by adding a new value attribute to the `<input/>` tags:

```
<input type="text" value="Type here to add task"/>
<input type="button" value="Add item"/>
```

Then we can change the CSS properties of our `<input/>` tags to make them look a bit more exciting. We do this with CSS classes, like we did in Mission 1. But this time, rather than giving our CSS class a name, we use the CSS type attribute selector to find and format our button. Let's have a look at the whole code block:

```
<!DOCTYPE html>
<html>
<head>
   <title>To-Do List App</title>
   <style>
     input[type="button"] {
        background-color: pink;
     }
   </style>
</head>
<body>
   <p>Special Exhibition To-Do List</p>
   <br/>
   <input type="text" value="Type here to add task"/>
   <br/>
   <input type="button" value="Add item"/>
   <br/>
</body>
</html>
```

This is the CSS type attribute selector. It finds the selected type attribute and then formats it to your chosen CSS properties

Type attribute

Special Exhibition To-Do List

Special Exhibition To-Do List

Type here to add task
Add item

Special Exhibition To-Do List

Type here to add task
Add item

But if you try to type into the text box or click the button, nothing will happen. If we want our button and text box to work, we need to add some JavaScript to our page.

CODE SKILLS ► HOW TO BUILD A BUTTON

Let's start making the app for Professor Bairstone by building a button. Use <input/> tags to code a text box and button.

1. Open up your text-editing program. Create a new HTML file called **app.html**. Type this code into your new file:

```
<!DOCTYPE html>
<html>
<head>
    <title>To-Do List App</title>
</head>
<body>
    <p>Special Exhibition To-Do List</p>
    <br/>
    <br/>
    <br/>
</body>
</html>
```

2. Now use the <input/> tag to create a text box and button in your <body>. Don't forget that you need to include two attributes inside your <input/> tags: the type and value attributes. You should set the value attribute to the text you want to display in your box and button. Your code will look like this:

```
<body>
    <p>Special Exhibition To-Do List</p>
    <br/>
    <input type="text" value="Type here to add task"/>
    <br/>
    <input type="button" value="Add item"/>
    <br/>
</body>
```

3. Save your HTML file and open it in your browser. You will see your box and button displayed on-screen.

    Now create a CSS class and use the CSS type attribute selector to change the colour of your button.

TO-DO LIST A ✖

    Special Exhibition To-Do List

    Type here to add task

    Add item

Making buttons run code

We now need to make the button in our app interactive. To make the button run JavaScript code when we click it, we need to add the onclick attribute to our button <input/> tag, like we did in Mission 2. When the user clicks on the button, we want it to call a JavaScript function. All we have to do is set the value of our onclick attribute to the name of the function we want to call.

Let's code a button that will call a function that pops up an alert when it's clicked. First create the JavaScript function you need. Then add the onclick attribute to the <input/> tag for the button. Finally set the value of the onclick attribute to the name of the function. Do this by using the equals sign (=) and double quotes (" "). The code we need looks like this:

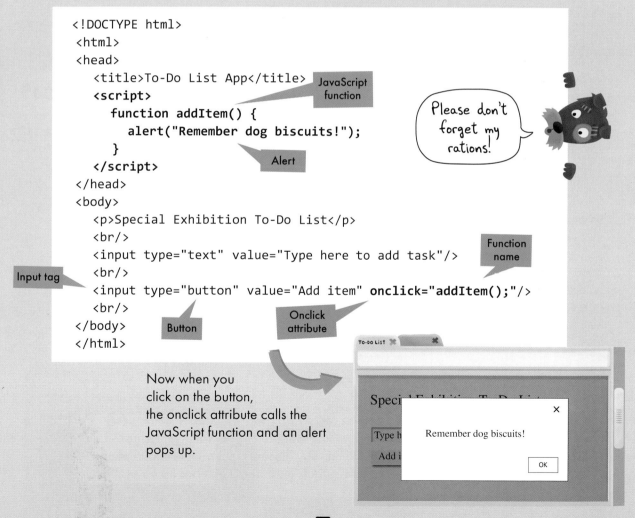

```
<!DOCTYPE html>
<html>
<head>
   <title>To-Do List App</title>          JavaScript function
   <script>
     function addItem() {
       alert("Remember dog biscuits!");
     }                            Alert
   </script>
</head>
<body>
   <p>Special Exhibition To-Do List</p>
   <br/>
   <input type="text" value="Type here to add task"/>    Function name
   <br/>
   <input type="button" value="Add item" onclick="addItem();"/>
   <br/>                    Onclick attribute
</body>        Button
</html>
```

Input tag

Please don't forget my rations!

Now when you click on the button, the onclick attribute calls the JavaScript function and an alert pops up.

Remember dog biscuits!

101

Using the DOM

The DOM API is structured in a special way called a "hierarchy", which is a bit like a family tree. This structure is called the document object. In the document object the individual HTML elements are all connected to each other, like the members of a family, with parents and children. The way the document object is structured allows you to use another programming language, such as JavaScript, to access, change, add or remove any of the HTML elements inside the document.

Using the DOM when you code allows you to make changes to individual HTML elements after they have been drawn on-screen. You can use the DOM's methods and properties to find a HTML element on your page and then, using JavaScript, add to it, remove it or change it.

If we want our app to be interactive, we need to learn how to use these methods and properties with JavaScript. Professor Bairstone needs to be able to see his tasks on-screen and then add and remove items.

DOM methods and properties

Before you can use any of the DOM's built-in functions, you have to tell your browser you want to access the API. To do this you always have to type this piece of code at the start of an instruction for the DOM.

Once you've told your browser you want to use the DOM, you then have to say which DOM functions you want to use. The DOM has built-in functions called methods and properties that allow you to change HTML elements. A method is an action you can do, such as adding or removing a HTML element. A property is a value that you can access and change, such as setting the contents of a HTML element to a piece of text.

When you want to use a method or property, you separate the DOM keyword from the DOM method or property with a dot (.). Because the DOM lets you access any HTML element in your web page, lots of DOM methods have the word "element" in them. In Mission 2 you used a DOM method with JavaScript when you wrote this code:

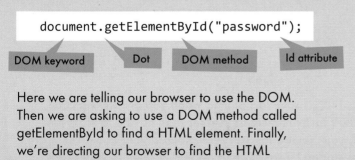

Here we are telling our browser to use the DOM. Then we are asking to use a DOM method called getElementById to find a HTML element. Finally, we're directing our browser to find the HTML element with that specific id attribute.

Did you notice?

When we use dots (.) to separate pieces of code we are using dot notation. The dot tells your browser you will be using DOM methods and properties.

104

changing your app with the DOM

We can use a DOM method to find a HTML element in our app by its id attribute. We can then use a DOM property to change the contents of that element. Let's take a look at how we do this.

Using the getElementById method

The getElementById method is a very handy way of finding a specific HTML element in your block of code. To use the getElementById method, you have to include the id attribute you gave to the HTML element in brackets after the keyword, like this:

```
document.getElementById("list");
```

DOM **Method keyword** **Id attribute you want to find**

Here we have asked our browser to find the HTML element in our web page that has the id attribute set to the value "list".

Using the innerHTML property

You can use the DOM's innerHTML property to access or change the contents of a HTML element in your app. You can then use the contents of the HTML element as a value in your JavaScript code.

Variable **HTML element**

```
var showList = document.getElementById("list");
alert(showList.innerHTML);
```

Alert **Id attribute** **innerHTML you want to set**

Here we have created a variable where the value is set to the contents of the HTML element that we have called "list", using the id attribute. We have then created an alert. The alert will pop up the value of our variable. Our browser can access this information because we have set the innerHTML property of the variable.

The DOM is case sensitive. Make sure your capital letters are in the right place.

Turn over to see how you can use this method and property.

105

Adding to your app using the DOM

We now know how to use the DOM's methods and properties to find and change HTML elements in our app, which will be really useful. We now need to learn how to use the DOM to add new HTML elements to our app. After all, Professor Bairstone needs to be able to add items to the list. The DOM has two methods that we can use with JavaScript to do this.

The createElement method

The createElement method is used to make a new HTML element, such as a <div>, button or a paragraph. You have to include the name of the type of HTML element you want to create in double quotes (" ") and brackets after the keyword, like this:

DOM | Method keyword | HTML element you want to create

```
document.createElement("div");
```

You can then use JavaScript to assign your new element to a variable, using the assignment operator (=) we learnt about in Mission 2. Then you can use the innerHTML property to set the content of your new element before your browser draws it on-screen.

The appendChild method

The appendChild method lets you add a new HTML element to an existing HTML element. When the new element is drawn on-screen, it will be drawn underneath the existing element. You have to include the HTML element you want to add in brackets after the keyword, like this:

Create <div>

```
<script>
   var newDiv = document.createElement("div");
   newDiv.innerHTML = "Professor Bairstone";
   document.body.appendChild(newDiv);
</script>
```

Set innerHTML

Location | appendChild

The appendChild and createElement methods allow you to add each item to the list in the app.

Did you notice?

All the DOM methods and properties are written using camelCase.

Let's have a look at an example that uses the createElement and appendChild methods to create a new HTML element on our page. The HTML element will be a <div> with a piece of text inside it. A <div> is a useful way of creating a section or container for other HTML elements.

```
<!DOCTYPE html>
<html>
<head>
   <title>To-Do List App</title>
</head>
<body>
   <div id="list">To-Do List</div>
   <script>
      var newItem = document.createElement("div");
      newItem.innerHTML = "Item added to list";
      document.getElementById("list").appendChild(newItem);
   </script>
</body>
</html>
```

Id attribute

createElement

Variable

Create <div>

appendChild

Add HTML element

The first thing we've done is code a <div> and set its id attribute to list. This <div> will be the HTML element we add our new HTML element to, using appendChild.

Then we've opened the <script> tag and created a block of JavaScript code. In the first line of JavaScript we have used createElement to make a <div>. We have then stored this new <div> in a variable called newItem. You can use any name you want here.

In our next line of JavaScript, we've set the value of our variable to a piece of text using the innerHTML property. Our new <div>, stored in our variable, now contains text.

TO-DO LIST

To-Do List
Item added to list

In our final line of JavaScript, we've used getElementById to find the first <div> we made using the id attribute. We've then used appendChild to add the <div> stored in our variable to the first <div> on our page.

When we run our code in our web browser, we will see our new <div> has been added to our first <div>.

You wouldn't believe how forgetful Professor Bairstone can be!

CODE SKILLS ► **ADDING NEW HTML ELEMENTS**

Now it's your turn to have a go at using the createElement and appendChild methods. In your code, use the DOM and JavaScript to create a new HTML element when an existing element is clicked. Using APIs like the DOM makes building apps easier.

1. Open up your text-editing program. Create a new HTML file called **newelements.html**. Code a <div> (with an id attribute) that contains text, like this:

```
<!DOCTYPE html>
<html>
<head>
    <title>New Elements</title>
</head>
<body>
    <div id="list">Click here to add item</div>
</body>
</html>
```

2. In your <head>, create a new function. Your code will look like this:

```
<head>
    <title>New Elements</title>
    <script>
      function addItem() {
      }
    </script>
</head>
```

3. Now make your function create a new <div> using the createElement method. Store your new <div> in a variable and give the variable a name. Then set the value of your new <div> to some text using the innerHTML property. Your code will look like this:

```
<script>
   function addItem() {
      var newItem = document.createElement("div");
      newItem.innerHTML = "New item";
   }
</script>
```

4. Add a final line to your function. Use getElementById to find the <div> in your <body>. Use the appendChild method to add the new <div> to the <div> in your <body>. Your code will look like this:

```
<script>
  function addItem() {
    var newItem = document.createElement("div");
    newItem.innerHTML = "New item";
    document.getElementById("list").appendChild(newItem);
  }
</script>
```

5. Now the only thing missing is the function call in the <body> of our code. Add the onclick attribute to the <div> in your <body>, so that when the <div> text is clicked your addItem function is called. Your code will look like this:

```
<body>
  <div id="list" onclick="addItem();">Click here to add item</div>
</body>
```

6. Save your HTML file and open it in your browser. When you click on the "Click here" piece of text a new <div> will be added to your app every time you click.

New Element

Click here to add item
New item
New item
New item
New item
New item
New item

But how do we add the button to the app?

Turn over to find out!

MAKING THE TO-DO LIST APP

Now you know what the DOM is and how it works, let's bring together all your new Code Skills and create the to-do list app. At the start of the mission you learnt how to build a text box and button using the `<input/>` tag. Let's take a look at that code again:

```
<!DOCTYPE html>
<html>
<head>
    <title>To-Do List App</title>
</head>
<body>
    <p>Special Exhibition To-Do List</p>
    <br/>
    <input type="text" value="Type here to add task"/>    ◀ Text box
    <br/>
    <input type="button" value="Add item"/>    ◀ Button
    <br/>
</body>
</html>
```

Special Exhibition To-Do List

Type here to add task

Add item

At the moment Professor Bairstone can type a task into the text box, but when he clicks on the button nothing happens. We have to use the DOM's methods and properties to add an item to the list when the button is clicked.

Let's start with the changes we need to make to our `<body>`. We need to add an onclick attribute to our `<input/>` tag to make our button work. This onclick has to call a function. We also need to create an empty `<div>` that will become our to-do list. When an item is added to the list, it will be added to this empty `<div>` using the DOM methods. Our `<body>` block will look like this:

```
<body>
  <p>Special Exhibition To-Do List</p>
  <br/>
  <input type="text" value="Type here to add task"/>
  <br/>
  <input type="button" value="Add item" onclick="addItem();"/>
  <br/>
  <div id="list"></div>
</body>
```

<div>

Onclick attribute

Now let's create a function in our <head> that will run when the onclick is clicked. Our function needs to use the createElement method to make a new <div>. This new <div> will be stored in a variable called newItem. Then we need to use innerHTML to set the text inside our newItem variable. Finally we need to use getElementById to find the <div> with the id attribute "list" in our body. Then we can use appendChild to add our newItem to our list. Our <script> block in our <head> will look like this:

```
<script>
  function addItem() {
    var newItem = document.createElement("div");
    newItem.innerHTML = "New item";
    document.getElementById("list").appendChild(newItem);
  }
</script>
```

Set innerHTML of new <div>

Create new <div>

Find id attribute

Add new <div> to <div> in <body>

When we run this code in our browser the button works. The text "New item" is added to the list every time the button is clicked.

To-Do List A

Special Exhibition To-Do List

Type here to add task

Add item

New item
New item
New item
New item

Now to make that text box work!

Adding your own tasks

Our app is really starting to take shape. Now an item is added to the list every time the user clicks the button. But Professor Bairstone can't yet type an item into the text box and add it to the list. Let's see how we can allow him to type in his own tasks.

We only need to change two lines in our code block to add the value of the text box to the list. The first thing we need to do is in our `<body>`. We need to give the `<input/>` tag for our text box an id attribute of our choice, like this:

Id attribute

```
<input type="text" id="box" value="Type here to add task"/>
```

We're then going to change our JavaScript in the `<head>` so that it sets the innerHTML of the new `<div>` to whatever value has been typed into the text box. To do that we have to use getElementById to find the text box using the id attribute. We then access the value by making this change to our `<script>` block:

```
<script>
  function addItem() {
    var newItem = document.createElement("div");
    newItem.innerHTML = document.getElementById("box").value;
    document.getElementById("list").appendChild(newItem);
  }
</script>
```

Id attribute

Access value

TO-DO List A

Special Exhibition To-Do List

Dog biscuits

Add item

Glass display case
Velvet cushion
Hire private security
Hire bodyguard
Invite guests
Snacks and lemonade

Now Professor Bairstone can replace the text in the text box with the item he wants to add to his list. Our addItem function will set whatever text is typed into the text box as the contents of the new `<div>`. He can now add his own items to the to-do list.

Gosh! There are so many things we need to do!

114

code skills checklist ✓

USING THE DOM API

- The DOM (or Document Object Model) is an API (Application Program Interface). When your HTML document runs in your web browser, it becomes part of the DOM called the document object. The way the document object is structured allows you to write code that will access and change individual HTML elements.

- You can use the DOM's built-in functions to make changes to HTML elements after they have been drawn on your screen. This is important if you want to make an interactive web page or web-based app that responds to the user.

- To access the DOM you have to type the document keyword. You also have to use dot (.) notation. Each new instruction for the DOM has to be separated by a dot.

- You can use DOM methods and properties to make changes to your HTML elements.

- getElementById is a DOM method that allows you to find a HTML element on your page by its id attribute.

- innerHTML is a DOM property. You can set the innerHTML of any HTML element. Using innerHTML is a good way to set or change the contents of a HTML element.

- createElement is a DOM method that lets you create a new HTML element. You have to tell your browser what type of element you want to create.

- appendChild is a DOM method that lets you add a new HTML element to an existing HTML element.

> The DOM saves you lots of time and makes it much easier to create a dynamic web page!

Removing from the app using the DOM

You know how to use the DOM to find and add HTML elements to your web page. But what happens if Professor Bairstone makes a mistake and adds the wrong item to the to-do list? Or if he completes a task and wants to remove it from the list? We need to learn how to remove HTML elements from our app using the DOM.

> Imagine if I added that new pair of woolly socks I need to the list! Terrible!

The removechild method

The removeChild method does the opposite to the appendChild method. Rather than adding a HTML element to another HTML element, it takes away a HTML element from another HTML element. You use it just like appendChild. Select the HTML element you want to remove using the id attribute and then tell your browser to remove it, like this:

Find parent HTML element

Remove child HTML element

```
document.getElementById("list").removeChild(this);
```

As you know already, HTML tags can be nested inside other HTML tags. When you use the removeChild method, you remove the HTML element inside the HTML element you selected using the id attribute.

> These new pieces of code are making our app more and more interactive.

In the document object all elements are connected, like in a family tree. Any HTML element that is inside another is called a child of that element. The HTML element on the outside is called the parent. When you use removeChild, you remove the child HTML element from the parent HTML element.

When you use the removeChild method you also have to use a handy JavaScript keyword called "this". The this keyword points to whichever HTML element was used to call the function. Let's take a look at an example:

```
<!DOCTYPE html>
<html>
<head>
  <title>Things To Buy</title>
  <script>
    function removeItem(item) {
      document.getElementById("list").removeChild(item);
    }
  </script>
</head>
<body>
  <div id="list">
      Velvet cushion for diamond
    <div onclick="removeItem(this);">
        Woolly socks
    </div>
  </div>
</body>
</html>
```

Argument

this keyword

Parent <div>

Child <div>

In this example, the first <div>, with the id attribute "list", is the parent element. The <div> nested inside it, with the woolly socks text, is the child element. When we click on the woolly socks text, we're using getElementById to find the <div> called list.

Then we're using the removeChild method and the this keyword to remove this piece of text. Just like we learnt in Mission 2, we have to pass an argument for our function to work. We use the argument "item" and the "this" keyword to keep track of the HTML element we are trying to remove. Professor Bairstone can now remove things from the list by clicking on them.

Things To

Velvet cushion for diamond
Woolly socks

Things To

Velvet cushion for diamond

Silly Professor Bairstone!

119

Let's have a go at using the removeChild method and this keyword to remove a HTML element.

1. Open up your text-editing program. Create a new HTML file called **remove.html**. Code a parent and a child <div> in your <body>. Set the id attribute of the parent <div>, like this:

```html
<!DOCTYPE html>
<html>
<head>
   <title>Remove Items</title>
</head>
<body>
   <div id="list">
      Security to protect Mr Volkov
      <div>
         Woolly socks
      </div>
   </div>
</body>
</html>
```

2. Now add a JavaScript function to your <head> that will remove the child <div> from your page. The function will find the parent <div> using the getElementById method. It will then use removeChild to remove the <div> nested inside it. Your code will look like this:

```html
<script>
   function removeItem(item) {
      document.getElementById("list").removeChild(item);
   }
</script>
```

3. Finally add an onclick attribute to the child <div>, so that when the text inside it is clicked, it will be removed from the list. The onclick should call your function and use the this keyword, like this:

```html
<div onclick="removeItem(this);">
   Woolly socks
</div>
```

4. Save your HTML file and open it in your browser. When you click on the second item, it will vanish from the screen.

Removing more than one HTML element

You're making great progress! Now you can remove a HTML element using the removeChild method. But what happens if Professor Bairstone wants to remove more than one item from his list? We need to use the DOM and JavaScript so that all the items can be removed from the list when they're clicked. To do this we need to add an onclick attribute every time we use the createElement method. You can use a DOM method to set the onclick by using the onclick keyword:

`.onclick`

We can then set our onclick to call a function that will remove the item when it is clicked, like this:

```
<!DOCTYPE html>
<html>
<head>
    <title>To-Do List App</title>
    <script>
      function addItem() {
        var newItem = document.createElement("div");
        newItem.innerHTML = document.getElementById("box").value;
        newItem.onclick = removeItem;
        document.getElementById("list").appendChild(newItem);
      }
      function removeItem() {
        document.getElementById("list").removeChild(this);
      }
    </script>
</head>
<body>
    <p>Special Exhibition To-Do List</p>
    <input type="text" id="box" value="Type here to add task"/>
    <br/>
    <input type="button" value="Add item" onclick="addItem();"/>
    <div id="list"></div>
</body>
</html>
```

We need to get all these tasks checked off the list!

Onclick attribute set

removeItem function called

In this example, we've created a new `<div>` using createElement. We've stored the `<div>` in a variable so we can set its innerHTML to whatever item has been typed into the text box. We then use the DOM to set the onclick attribute of the new item. When this item is clicked, it will call the removeItem function and the item will be removed from the list.

Use your new knowledge to make an app where more than one HTML element can be removed when it's clicked. Every new skill you learn is making your app more advanced.

1. Open up your text-editing program. Create a new HTML file called **removemore.html**. Copy and paste your code from **basicapp.html**. Your code will look like this:

> I've got a bone to pick with those Bond Brothers! All this planning!

```
<!DOCTYPE html>
<html>
<head>
   <title>To-Do List App</title>
   <script>
     function addItem() {
        var newItem = document.createElement("div");
        newItem.innerHTML = document.getElementById("box").value;
        document.getElementById("list").appendChild(newItem);
     }
   </script>
</head>
<body>
   <p>Special Exhibition To-Do List</p>
   <br/>
   <input type="text" id="box" value="Type here to add task"/>
   <br/>
   <input type="button" value="Add item" onclick="addItem();"/>
   <br/>
   <div id="list"></div>
</body>
</html>
```

2. Now modify your addItem function in your <head> by setting up the onclick attribute in your function. Add an onclick to every new HTML element. Make your onclick call a new function when it is clicked. Add this new line of code to your <script> block:

```
<script>
   function addItem() {
      var newItem = document.createElement("div");
      newItem.innerHTML = document.getElementById("box").value;
      newItem.onclick = removeItem;
      document.getElementById("list").appendChild(newItem);
   }
</script>
```

3. Code a second function in your <script> block called removeItem. The function needs to use getElementById to find the <div> in your <body>. Then it should use removeChild and the this keyword to remove any item the function calls. Type out this function so your <script> block now looks like this:

```
<script>
   function addItem() {
      var newItem = document.createElement("div");
      newItem.innerHTML = document.getElementById("box").value;
      newItem.onclick = removeItem;
      document.getElementById("list").appendChild(newItem);
   }
   function removeItem() {
      document.getElementById("list").removeChild(this);
   }
</script>
```

I'm Viktor Volkov. It's great to meet you. I can't tell you how grateful I am for your help. Your coding skills are very impressive.

PTO

4. Your finished code block for your app will look like this:

```
<!DOCTYPE html>
<html>
<head>
   <title>To-Do List App</title>
   <script>
      function addItem() {
         var newItem = document.createElement("div");
         newItem.innerHTML = document.getElementById("box").value;
         newItem.onclick = removeItem;
         document.getElementById("list").appendChild(newItem);
      }
      function removeItem() {
         document.getElementById("list").removeChild(this);
      }
   </script>
</head>
<body>
   <p>Special Exhibition To-Do List</p>
   <br/>
   <input type="text" id="box" value="Type here to add task"/>
   <br/>
   <input type="button" value="Add item" onclick="addItem();"/>
   <br/>
   <div id="list"></div>
</body>
</html>
```

This special exhibition is going to be a blast!

Save your HTML file and open it in your browser. You can now add and remove items from the list.

TO-DO Li✱

Special Exhibition To-Do List

| Add item |
Glass display case
Velvet cushion
Hire private security
Woolly socks
Snacks and lemonade

TO-DO Li✱

Special Exhibition To-Do List

| Add item |
Glass display case
Velvet cushion
Hire private security
Snacks and lemonade

SAVING YOUR TO-DO LIST ITEMS

Professor Bairstone can now add and remove as many items as he needs from the list. But you might have noticed that if you refresh your page, your to-do list disappears. This is because so far we've just added or removed HTML elements from our screen. We haven't saved the list or changed our HTML file. If we want our browser to save and remember our list, we need to use localStorage, a handy API that's available in HTML5 (the fifth version of the HTML programming language).

This API lets you save information in your browser, so even if your page is refreshed or closed you can still access the data. Like the DOM, localStorage is a collection of functions, and it's simple to use.

All you have to do is tell your browser you want to use localStorage by typing the localStorage keyword (written in camelCase) and giving a name to the information you want to store. Set the value of the information you want to store using an equals sign (=) and double quotes (" "), like this:

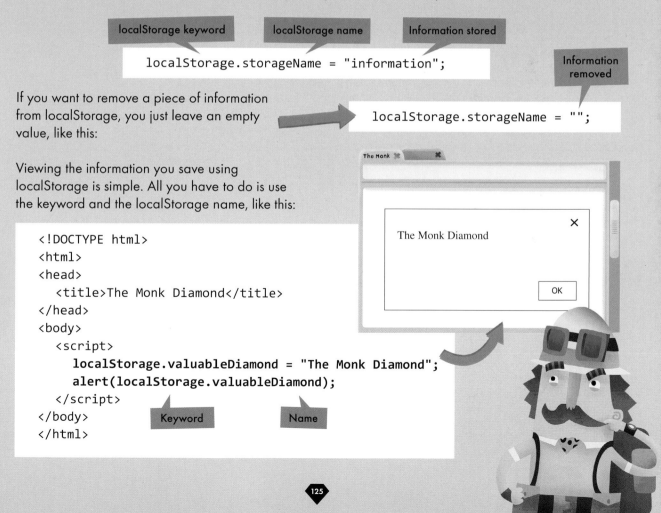

localStorage keyword | localStorage name | Information stored

```
localStorage.storageName = "information";
```

If you want to remove a piece of information from localStorage, you just leave an empty value, like this:

Information removed

```
localStorage.storageName = "";
```

Viewing the information you save using localStorage is simple. All you have to do is use the keyword and the localStorage name, like this:

```
<!DOCTYPE html>
<html>
<head>
   <title>The Monk Diamond</title>
</head>
<body>
   <script>
     localStorage.valuableDiamond = "The Monk Diamond";
     alert(localStorage.valuableDiamond);
   </script>
</body>
</html>
```

Keyword | Name

The Monk Diamond

OK

CODE SKILLS ► **USING THE LOCALSTORAGE API**

Let's have a go at using localStorage to store information in our web browser. This way the list in Professor Bairstone's app will be safely stored.

1. Open up your text-editing program. Create a new HTML file called **storage.html**. Type this code into the <body> of your new file:

```
<!DOCTYPE html>
<html>
<head>
   <title>Storage</title>
</head>
<body>
   <input type="text" id="box" value="Type here to add task"/><br/>
   <input type="button" id="save" value="Save" onclick="save();"/><br/>
   <input type="button" id="load" value="Load" onclick="load();"/><br/>
   Saved item: <div id="savedList"></div>
</body>
</html>
```

2. Now code a function in your <head> that uses localStorage to save the value typed into the text box in your browser. Don't forget to use camelCase when you write the localStorage keyword. Your code will look like this:

```
<script>
   function save() {
      var newItem = document.getElementById("box").value;
      localStorage.box = newItem;
   }
</script>
```

> Don't forget to use Google Chrome or Mozilla Firefox for this exercise.

3. Now code a second function in your `<script>` block that uses the getElementById method to find your empty `<div>`. Use innerHTML to set the value of your empty `<div>` to the information you saved using localStorage. Make sure your function looks like this:

```
<script>
   function save() {
      var newItem = document.getElementById("box").value;
      localStorage.box = newItem;
   }
   function load() {
      var savedDiv = document.getElementById("savedList");
      savedDiv.innerHTML = localStorage.box;
   }
</script>
```

4. Save your HTML file and open it in your browser. Type something into the text box and click *Save*.

5. Now click *Load*. The value you typed into the text box will appear on-screen. Then refresh your page. The item will disappear from your screen. But when you press *Load*, the text you saved using localStorage will be loaded in your browser.

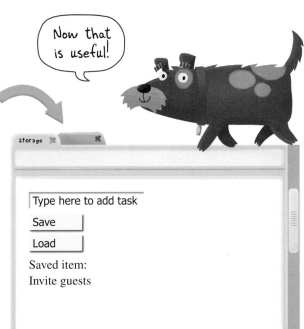

Did you notice?

When writing the localStorage keyword we use camelCase. The first letter is lower-case and the second word starts with an upper-case letter.

Saving and loading using localStorage

Now you know about localStorage, let's look at how we can use it to save and load Professor Bairstone's app. Every time Professor Bairstone changes the to-do list, it needs to save in localStorage. We also need to write code that will load the to-do list from localStorage when Professor Bairstone opens it in his browser. Let's take a look at the changes we need to make to our `<script>` block to use localStorage like this:

```
<!DOCTYPE html>
<html>
<head>
  <title>To-Do List App</title>
  <script>
    function addItem() {
      var newItem = document.createElement("div");
      newItem.innerHTML = document.getElementById("box").value;
      newItem.onclick = removeItem;
      document.getElementById("list").appendChild(newItem);
      saveList();                      Save list function call
    }
    function removeItem() {
      document.getElementById("list").removeChild(this);
      saveList();              Save list function call        List saved to
    }                                                          localStorage
    function saveList() {
      localStorage.storedList = document.getElementById("list").innerHTML;
    }
    function loadList() {
      document.getElementById("list").innerHTML = localStorage.storedList;
    }
    </script>
</head>
<body>
  <p>Special Exhibition To-Do List</p>
  <input type="text" id="box" value="Type here to add task"/>
  <br/>
  <input type="button" value="Add item" onclick="addItem();"/>
  <div id="list"></div>
</body>
</html>
```

Save list function

Load list function

128

Saving the list

To save the list we need to create a new saveList function that will save it using localStorage. To do this, we have to choose a variable name to assign the information we want to store in localStorage. We then use getElementById to find the <div> in the <body> of our page. Finally we use innerHTML to get the contents of the <div>. Everything in our <div> will now be saved in localStorage.

We want to save our list every time an item is added or removed, so we also need to make sure the addItem and removeItem functions call the saveList function after they have run.

Loading the list

To load the list we need to create a second function. Whenever the loadList function is called, it will set the innerHTML of the <div> with the id "list" to whatever has been saved in localStorage.

We need to call our loadList function so that when our browser finishes loading, it loads our list too. To make sure we don't try to load a list that hasn't been saved, we have to use an if statement before we try to use localStorage. The if statement we need looks like this:

```
<div id="list"></div>
<script>
  if(localStorage.storedList) {
    loadList();
  }
</script>
```

Load list function call

The if statement checks if there is a list saved in localStorage before trying to load it. When we save our complete code block and run our app in our browser, items we add to the list are now saved even if we close and then reopen our file.

Without this if statement our saved list won't load.

Removing from localStorage

There's just one more thing we have to do to make our loadList function work properly. At the moment when you use the to-do list app, you'll be able to add and remove items by clicking on an item. But if you load your saved list from localStorage, you won't be able to remove an item when you click on it.

This is because we're only saving the HTML elements into localStorage, not the onclick attribute that we add when each element is created. We need to add the onclick attribute back to each of our list items, so that the removeItem function still works after we load our list from localStorage. We need to add one final piece of code to our loadList function in our <head>, so it looks like this:

```
function loadList() {
    document.getElementById("list").innerHTML = localStorage.storedList;
    for(var i = 0; i < list.children.length; i++) {
        list.children[i].onclick = removeItem;
    }
}
```

Code that starts the loop

Code to run in loop

Condition for loop

We've now added a **loop** to our loadList function. This loop adds our onclick attribute to our removeItem function on every item that we load from localStorage. It counts up through each new HTML element that we've added to our to-do list and sets the onclick attribute for each new element.

You will learn more about loops in Mission 5, but for now you should know that loops are split into three parts.

CODE WORDS A **LOOP** is a special piece of JavaScript that runs the same piece of code again and again. Programmers use them so they don't have to type the same piece of code over and over.

A loop needs:

- ♦ **The code that starts the loop**
- ♦ **The condition to check if the loop is allowed to run**
- ♦ **Code that runs every time the loop runs.**

That's very clever coding!

DO IT YOURSELF TASK
BUILD A TO-DO LIST APP

Now use all the new skills you've learnt in this mission to build the to-do list app Professor Bairstone needs for the Monk Diamond special exhibition. Use JavaScript with the DOM and localStorage APIs to make a to-do-list that Professor Bairstone can add items to. Make sure that when he completes a task he can click on the item to remove it from the list.

The TO-DO List App Brief

When you code your app use HTML and JavaScript and the new APIs. Make sure you include these things:

- **A function that adds an item to the list, using the DOM**
- **A function that removes an item from the list, using the DOM**
- **A function that saves the list, using localStorage**
- **A function that loads the list, using localStorage**
- **A text box the user can type the items into**
- **A button that the user can click to add an item to the list**

Save your file in your **Coding** folder and call it **listapp.html**.

Turn over to see the entire code block you need for your app!

Don't forget to use the Get Coding! website if you need help.

```
<!DOCTYPE html>
<html>
<head>
   <title>To-Do List App</title>
   <script>
     function addItem() {
        var newItem = document.createElement("div");
        newItem.innerHTML = document.getElementById("box").value;
        newItem.onclick = removeItem;
        document.getElementById("list").appendChild(newItem);
        saveList();
     }
     function removeItem() {
        document.getElementById("list").removeChild(this);
        saveList();
     }
     function saveList() {
        localStorage.storedList = document.getElementById("list").innerHTML;
     }
     function loadList() {
        document.getElementById("list").innerHTML = localStorage.storedList;
        for(var i = 0; i < list.children.length; i++) {
           list.children[i].onclick = removeItem;
        }
     }
   </script>
</head>
```

This special exhibition is going to be fantastic. I can't wait!

132

```
<body>
  <p>The House of Volkov</p>
  <p>Special Exhibition To-Do List</p>
  <br/>
  <input type="text" id="box" value="Type here to add task"/>
  <br/>
  <input type="button" value="Add item" onclick="addItem();"/>
  <br/>
  <div id="list"></div>
  <script>
    if(localStorage.storedList) {
       loadList();
    }
  </script>
</body>
</html>
```

Now use CSS to change the design of your app so it looks like this!

FUTURE CODE SKILLS

Using APIs like the DOM and localStorage when you're coding with HTML, CSS and JavaScript allows you to create more complex and interactive web pages or web-based apps. Now you can use the DOM to access some powerful features in your browser. It allows you to dynamically make changes to the HTML as your user interacts with your page or app. Great work!

MISSION 4

PLAN A ROUTE

- ◆ **LEARN HOW TO ADD CONTENT FROM ANOTHER WEB PAGE**

- ◆ **EMBED A MAP IN YOUR PAGE USING A WEB API**

- ◆ **USE AN API KEY**

- ◆ **LEARN HOW THE ‹IFRAME› TAG WORKS**

- ◆ **PLAN A ROUTE USING GOOGLE MAPS**

Mission Brief

Dear Coder,

You will be pleased to hear that we have finally made it to Moscow after a long train journey. We are currently lying low at a secret location, as we want no one but Mr Volkov to know we've arrived in the city with the Monk Diamond. Mr Volkov came to see us – he's a charming man. I'm so happy we've found his lost jewel.

He and Professor Bairstone have been extremely busy getting everything ready for the exhibition. Your app has been very helpful and so far everything is going according to plan. There is only one thing that Professor Bairstone and Mr Volkov haven't thought of: how do we safely transport the diamond from our secret location to the House of Volkov?

The Bond Brothers have been known to ambush and rob courier vans transporting expensive jewellery in daring heists. I'm sending you an entry from the Explorer's Encyclopedia so you can see what I mean. We could deliver the diamond to the shop ourselves, but Professor Bairstone is such a famous figure I'm worried we will draw attention to ourselves and therefore the exhibition plans.

We've decided that the best thing to do would be for me to take the diamond to the nearby **Gorky Park**. Mr Volkov's head of security will be waiting for me and together we will take the diamond to the House of Volkov, which is right next to **St Basil's Cathedral**. Would you be able to help us by planning a route through the city? It will be really helpful to have a web page with a map embedded in it. It would be terrible if we got lost or were duped by the Bond Brothers into going the wrong way. Imagine if we lost the Monk Diamond now!

Thank you for helping us again. Everything is so nearly ready. We've just had the invitations for the exhibition printed and they are now ready to be sent to the guests. I'm sending you one too!

Very best wishes from our city hideaway,
Dr Ruby Day

THE EXPLORER'S ENCYCLOPEDIA
The Guide to Every Adventure

The Bond Brothers' Robberies

From the Explorer's Encyclopedia, the guide to every adventure

For other jewel thieves, see Famous Jewel Thieves.

The **Bond Brothers' Robberies** are the audacious jewel thefts carried out by the gang of <u>jewel thieves</u> known as the <u>Bond Brothers</u>. The majority of the <u>jewels</u> taken in their raids have never been seen again. Normally stolen jewellery is sold on the <u>black market</u> soon after a theft, but the Bond Brothers are thought to have a top secret hiding place for their loot.

*Mr V. Volkov requests the pleasure
of your company*

*at a very special exhibition hosted by
the House of Volkov*

*on 21 June at 7.00 p.m. at
the House of Volkov, near to
St Basil's Cathedral, Moscow.*

*You are invited to meet guests of honour
Professor Bairstone, Dr Day
and Ernest*

*and to hear about the sensational discovery
made on their recent expedition.*

RSVP

Interpol know that the gang has three core members, who are known only by their aliases: Light Fingers, Gemma the Gem and Tony Twinkles. The three members are aided by other smaller crooks, who help them choose their targets, make their escapes and hide the stolen jewels.

One of the gang is a skilled cyber-criminal, with access to government databases. In all their robberies the CCTV cameras in the area surrounding the target are disabled during the period of the crime.

As well as stealing from expensive boutiques in smash-and-grab raids, the Bond Brothers have held up courier vans or motorcycles delivering jewellery. They have disguised themselves as road workers and then used fake road signs to direct the drivers into dead-end roads, before robbing them.

Their success seems to be due to the way they vary their tactics. No raid is ever the same, making it very hard for the authorities to predict what they will do next.

ADDING CONTENT USING A WEB API

Now you've read the Mission Brief and know what Dr Day needs you to do, let's get coding! This will be a bit different to what you've done in the other three missions, but don't worry. The great thing about learning how to build web pages or apps that use the Internet is that you don't always have to do the hard work yourself.

It might sound a challenge to create a web page with a map **embedded** in it, but we don't have to code the map from scratch. All we have to do is write some code to call a URL on the Internet that has the map we need. Programmers call this integrating one web page with another.

When we want to integrate our web page with another website, we have to write some code that will connect our page to the web server that stores the other website. We can then access the data and content on that server that we need.

CODE WORDS

When a new piece of content is inserted into an existing web page, we say it has been **EMBEDDED** in the page. The embedded content becomes part of the page.

Web APIs

You already know what an API is and have used two of them in Mission 3: the DOM and localStorage APIs. Those APIs let you access some handy built-in functions. APIs come in all shapes and sizes and the API that we need to embed a map in this mission is slightly different to those we have used already.

APIs used to integrate with other websites are sometimes called "web APIs" or "web services". They let you access a website's built-in features and functions, so you can add extra content to your page without having to write lots of code.

You can use web APIs for lots of different things when you're building a website. You might have come across some of these web APIs on websites, which help you do these things:

- **Add maps**
- **Add *Like* or *Share* buttons for Facebook**
- **Share videos on YouTube and Twitch**

Web APIs let everyone build better and more complex websites quickly and easily. To embed a map and plan a route we are going to use a map web API.

There are several websites on the Internet that let you embed their maps on your web pages. Most of them even let you do it for free. The most popular free map web APIs are Google Maps and Bing

Maps, which are run by Google and Microsoft.

We're going to learn how you can use Google Maps to find the best route for Dr Day and the House of Volkov's head of security. You've probably used Google Maps before to look up an address, but this time you are going to learn how to program your very own map and then embed it in your web page.

Map web APIS

To use the Google Maps web API you have to register with Google and get a special piece of code called an API key. An API key is a special password that your web page uses to access the Google Maps API on the Google server. If you don't use an API key you won't be able to embed a map. You can get a Google Maps API key by visiting:

```
https://developers.google.com/maps/documentation/embed/
```

An API key is a long piece of code made up of letters and numbers. Every one is different, but will look something like this:

Did you know?

You need a Google account to get a Google Maps API key. You have to be over 13 years old to have a Google account. If you are under 13, ask an adult if you can use their account with their supervision, or if they can sign up on your behalf. Make sure you, or the adult helping you, have read the terms and conditions. Go to **www.support.google.com** to find out more.

Turn over to find out how to get your own API key.

CODE SKILLS ► GETTING A GOOGLE MAPS API KEY

Let's learn how you can get a Google Maps API key. You'll need it later in the mission to create the route for Dr Day.

1. Start by going to the Google Maps API website. Type this link into your browser:

```
https://developers.google.com/maps/documentation/embed/
```

2. Find the *GET A KEY* button. Click on it.

3. You'll see a pop-up with three options. Click *CONTINUE*.

4. Now sign into a Google account. Remember if you are under 13 you need to get an adult to help you. You will be sent to the Google Developers Console. Make sure you (if you are over the age requirement), or the adult helping you, have read the terms and conditions. You need to agree to them in order to proceed. Then select *Create a new project* from the drop-down list and click *Continue*.

5. You will then be asked to create an API key. Don't fill anything in – just click *Create*.

6. Your API key will be displayed. It will be a long code made up of numbers and letters. They are all unique but it will look a bit like this:

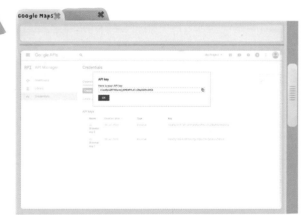

7. Now copy and paste your API key into your text-editing program. Save your file in your **Coding** folder as a text file (use the extension **.txt**). Call your new file **APIkey.txt**.

Coder, take note! Some of these steps might change as Google updates its software.

Keep your API key safe as you'll need it later in the mission!

HOW TO EMBED CONTENT

Now you know what embedding is and you've got an API key for Google Maps, we can start making our web page for Dr Day. We first need to learn how to embed content from another website in our web page. To do this we need to learn some new HTML tags and attributes.

The <iframe> tag: <iframe> and </iframe>

To add a Google Map to our page, we need to use a new HTML tag called the <iframe> tag. The opening tag is <iframe> and the closing tag is </iframe>. The tag is used to create an inline frame, which is a really useful way of embedding content from another website in your page. You can also use several attributes with the tag to change the way your embedded content displays.

The first attribute you have to include is the source (src) attribute, which we used in Mission 1. The source attribute tells your browser which piece of content you want to embed and is in the form of a URL. When you are integrating your website the information in the URL is very important for your browser. Let's take a look at an example with the Monk Diamond Discovery page:

```
<!DOCTYPE html>
<html>
<head>
   <title>Diamond Discovery</title>
</head>
                    Source attribute
<body>
   <iframe src="https://www.monkdiamonddiscovery.com">
   </iframe>
</body>
</html>
```

<iframe>

URL

A small section of the Monk Diamond Discovery web page that we provided as a URL will appear embedded in your page. However it's quite hard to see the embedded page at this small size. You need to include some other attributes inside your opening <iframe> tag to change the size, shape and appearance of the embedded page. Let's take a look at all the attributes you can use:

The Monk Diamond Disc

Stolen Diamond Discovered in Sib

Professor Bairstone and Dr Day have made a sensational discovery.
They have discovered the Monk Diamond in a remote cave in Siberia.

Attribute name	What does it do?	Example values
src	Provides the URL for the piece of content you want to embed	http://www.bing.com
width	Sets the maximum width of the `<iframe>`	600px; 20%
height	Sets the maximum height of the `<iframe>`	600px; 20%
frameborder	Sets the width of the border around the `<iframe>`	0px; 4px
style	Sets the style of the `<iframe>` using a CSS property and value	border: 0px

Now let's see how we can use all these attributes to change the appearance of our `<iframe>` and embedded content. Remember you always have to add attributes inside your opening tag, like this:

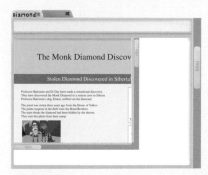

```
<!DOCTYPE html>
<html>
<head>
    <title>Diamond Discovery</title>
</head>
<body>
    <iframe
        width="350px"          Width attribute
        height="350px"          Frameborder attribute
        frameborder="0px"
        style="border: 0px"     Style attribute
        src="https://www.monkdiamonddiscovery.com">
    </iframe>
</body>
</html>
```
Height attribute

Useful thing, this `<iframe>` tag!

Here we've set the width and height attributes to the same number of pixels to make our `<iframe>` into a square. The frameborder attribute and the CSS border property have both been set to 0 pixels. This is so the `<iframe>` will blend into the page. You normally do this with an `<iframe>`, so that the embedded content looks like it is part of your page.

Now you've read about the `<iframe>` tag and how it works, let's have a go at using the tag and its attributes to change the way a piece of embedded content displays in a web page.

1. Open up your text-editing program. Create a new HTML file called **iframe.html**. Add the opening and closing `<iframe>` tags to the `<body>` of your page, so the code in your new file looks like this:

```
<!DOCTYPE html>
<html>
<head>
    <title>iFrames</title>
</head>
<body>
    <iframe>
    </iframe>
</body>
</html>
```

2. Now set the attributes of your `<iframe>`. Include the width, height, frameborder and style attribute inside your opening `<iframe>` tag, like this:

```
<body>
    <iframe
        width="350px"
        height="350px"
        frameborder="0px"
        style="border: 0px">
    </iframe>
</body>
```

3. Finally add the source attribute. Set its value to the URL of your favourite website, like this:

```
<iframe
    width="350px"
    height="350px"
    frameborder="0px"
    style="border: 0px"
    src="https://www.bing.com">
</iframe>
```

4. Save your HTML file and open it in your browser. Your chosen site will be embedded in your web page.

Now try changing the height and width of your `<iframe>` and seeing what it does to the embedded content.

I really like this way of embedding new content in our page.

EMBEDDING A GOOGLE MAP

As you can see, the `<iframe>` tag is really useful. Let's learn now how we can integrate a Google Map into our page using it. The simplest kind of Google Map you can add is called an embedded search. You use a Google API called the Google Maps Embed API. When the user gives the API a keyword, such as the name of a country, city or street, it will produce a map based on that keyword.

URLS

The Google Maps Embed API needs you to provide it with a URL in the source attribute of your `<iframe>`. The URL has to contain several important pieces of information so the correct map is embedded. Let's have a look at exactly what information we need to include in a URL if we want to embed a map of Moscow in our web page:

API key

```
https://www.google.com/maps/embed/v1/search?q=Moscow&key=API-KEY
```

Path   Search API function   Query string parameters

The first part of the URL is the path to the Google Maps Embed API. You then have to tell that API what built-in function you want to use. We want to use the search API function on the Google server, so we add that to the URL. The next piece of information is the specific part of our request, called the query **string parameters**.

CODE WORDS

A **STRING** is a piece of data in the form of a sequence of characters. Strings can be made up of words and numbers.

A **PARAMETER** is another name for a piece of information, or an argument, that is passed to a function so it can perform an action.

string parameters

The string parameters are the parts of a URL that contain variables – the pieces of information that depend on the user. In our example there are two parameters. The two variables are the map we are searching for (Moscow) and our unique API key.

We have to structure our query string parameters in a certain way, so the Google server is able to access information stored in our variables. The two parts of the query string parameters are the key and the value. You need both of these parts for your parameters to work. Turn over to see the URL for the map of Moscow.

```
https://www.google.com/maps/embed/v1/search?q=Moscow&key=API-KEY
```

Key   Value   Key   Value

In this URL the two parameters are separated by an ampersand (&). The first is the query key and the second is the API key. Your browser needs them both because they contain this important information:

Parameter key	What does it do?	Example value
q	Gives the location you want to search for	Moscow; London
key	Gives the API key needed to access the Google server	API-KEY

The Google Maps Embed API needs these two parameters to find the map we want to embed and then to integrate it into our page. Let's see what happens if we use these two parameters in our URL and set it as the source attribute for our `<iframe>`. When we save our file and open it in our browser, we will see a map of Moscow embedded in our page.

```
<!DOCTYPE html>
<html>
<head>
  <title>Moscow</title>
</head>
<body>
  <iframe
    width="450px"
    height="450px"
    frameborder="0px"
    style="border: 0px"
    src="https://www.google.com/maps/embed/v1/search?q=Moscow&key=API-KEY">
  </iframe>
</body>
</html>
```

CODE SKILLS ► EMBED A GOOGLE MAP

Let's embed a Google Map for Moscow in a page. It's an important skill to master before we plan our route for Dr Day and the head of security.

1. Open up your text-editing program. Create a new HTML file called **citymap.html**. Then copy and paste your code from **iframe.html** into your new file. Modify it so that it looks like this:

```
<!DOCTYPE html>
<html>
<head>
    <title>City Map</title>
</head>
<body>
    <iframe>
    </iframe>
</body>
</html>
```

2. Now add the width, height, frameborder and style attributes inside your opening `<iframe>` tag. Set the values, like this:

```
<body>
    <iframe
        width="450px"
        height="450px"
        frameborder="0px"
        style="border: 0px">
    </iframe>
</body>
```

3. Add the source attribute inside your opening `<iframe>` tag. Use the Google Maps Embed API URL and add the two parameters. Set the parameter "q" to the location you want for your map and the parameter "key" to your unique API key that you got earlier in the mission. Your source attribute will look like this:

```
<iframe
    width="450px"
    height="450px"
    frameborder="0px"
    style="border: 0px"
    src="https://www.google.com/maps/embed/
        v1/search?q=Moscow&key=API-KEY">
</iframe>
```

4. Save your HTML file and open it in your browser. You will see your map embedded in your page.

PLAN A ROUTE USING GOOGLE MAPS

Now we know how to embed a map in our page, we can start planning the route Dr Day and the head of security need to take through Moscow. To do this, we need to build a new URL and use a new function in the Google Maps Embed API. We have to create our URL in a slightly different way.

We need to use the directions function, rather than the search function. The directions function will create a map that gives a route from a specified location to another specified location. Dr Day needs to take the Monk Diamond from Gorky Park to St Basil's Cathedral, so our new URL will look like this:

Path

Directions API function

String parameters

```
https://www.google.com/maps/embed/v1/directions?
origin=GorkyPark,Moscow&destination=StBasil,Moscow&key=API-KEY
```

Like before, the first part of our URL is the path to the Google Maps Embed API. We then request to use the directions API function. Then we use three parameters: the origin, destination and API key. For the origin and destination you can put lots of different values, but the simplest thing to do is put the place name followed by the city name. These two new keys are important for your browser as they provide the following information:

Parameter key	What does it do?	Example value
origin	Gives the place you want your route to start	GorkyPark,Moscow
destination	Gives the place you want your route to end	StBasil,Moscow

Did you notice?

We've included the name of the site and the city, separated by a comma (,). There is no space after the comma.

I can't wait to see St Basil's Cathedral!

Let's add our new URL to our source attribute and see the route Dr Day and the head of security need to take through Moscow:

```
<!DOCTYPE html>
<html>
<head>
   <title>Top Secret Route</title>
</head>
<body>
   <iframe
      width="650px"
      height="650px"
      frameborder="0px"
      style="border: 0px"
      src="https://www.google.com/maps/embed/v1/directions?
         origin=GorkyPark,Moscow&destination=StBasil,Moscow&key=
         API-KEY">
   </iframe>
</body>
</html>
```

> This is exactly what Dr Day needs to get the Monk Diamond safely to the House of Volkov!

149

DO IT YOURSELF TASK
PLAN A ROUTE

Great work! You've learnt how to use a web API and Google Maps to embed content in your page. Now use your new knowledge to plan a route through Moscow, from Gorky Park to St Basil's Cathedral. Having a route will help Dr Day keep the Monk Diamond safe.

Moscow Route Planning Brief

When you plan your route, use your new Code Skills to do the following things:

- **Use an API key**: use the Google Maps Embed API to get an API key.

- **Create an `<iframe>`**: use this new HTML tag so you can embed content in your page.

- **Change the way your `<iframe>` displays**: use attributes to change the height, width and borders of your `<iframe>`.

- **Use the source attribute**: embed a URL that will connect to the web API you need.

- **Use the Google Maps Embed API**: create a Google Map using the Google API.

- **Use the built-in direction function**: plot a route using this function.

- **Set query string parameters**: give the destination function the origin and destination for your route.

Save your file in your **Coding** folder and call it **route.html**.

Don't forget to use your saved API key.

```
<!DOCTYPE html>
<html>
<head>
   <title>Top Secret Route</title>
</head>
<body>
   <iframe
     width="1000px"
     height="1000px"
     frameborder="0px"
     style="border: 0px"
     src="https://www.google.com/maps/embed/v1/directions?
        origin=GorkyPark,Moscow&destination=StBasil,Moscow&key=API-KEY">
   </iframe>
</body>
</html>
```

FUTURE CODE SKILLS

Knowing how to use web APIs means you can easily include features from other apps or websites in your code. You can use them to build pages and apps that use big web services, such as social networks like Facebook or Instagram, or utilities like Google Maps or Dropbox. This will save you time and stop you having to code functions from scratch.

This is what your finished code will look like!

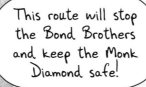

This route will stop the Bond Brothers and keep the Monk Diamond safe!

MAKE A GAME

- **USE TIMERS IN JAVASCRIPT**

- **LEARN WHAT GAME LOOPS ARE AND HOW THEY WORK**

- **LEARN HOW TO ANIMATE HTML ELEMENTS WITH JAVASCRIPT**

- **BUILD A GAME THAT TESTS REACTION TIMES**

Dear Coder,

The Monk Diamond arrived at the House of Volkov yesterday. Dr Day and I are both so grateful for your help with planning the route. All seemed to go smoothly, although Dr Day did think a bearded man, wearing a large hat, might have been following them. He vanished quickly, but she was slightly alarmed. Thank goodness the diamond arrived safely.

It's been positioned in its new glass case, on its new cushion, and it looks dazzling! We've just been arranging the snacks on silver platters, which was the final task on our list. Everything is now ready for the grand opening of the exhibition tonight.

Between you and me, ever since the incident with the boulder I have been worried about our security arrangements. I know we have been very careful to keep the discovery of the Monk Diamond a secret and you did a great job creating a password for our web page. But I am worried the Bond Brothers might still be on our trail (don't forget we think one of them is a skilled cyber-criminal). My biggest fear is that they could sabotage the exhibition by stealing the diamond again.

An old pal in London, who works for one of the city's most famous museums, recently told me she has trained a superb new security team using a computer game. I didn't believe her until she showed me the data. The game sharpened the team's reaction times significantly, and they responded to suspicious circumstances at the museum far more quickly than they had before they played the game.

I was wondering if you could help me by building a game that will test the reaction times of the House of Volkov's security team? I'm tied up this afternoon, as I still need to buy Ernest a new collar, so I was really hoping you could help. I've attached one of my private entries on the Explorer's Encyclopedia. It contains sensitive information about the exhibition, so please don't share it with anyone.

Thank you again for your excellent help. Warmest wishes from bustling Moscow,
Professor Harry Bairstone

The House of Volkov's Security Team

THE EXPLORER'S ENCYCLOPEDIA
The Guide to Every Adventure

From the Explorer's Encyclopedia, the guide to every adventure

This is a private entry with restricted access. To view the public entry for the House of Volkov click here.

The **House of Volkov's Security Team** is responsible for protecting the highly valuable jewels on display in the House of Volkov's private collection.

Since the theft of the Monk Diamond, the jewels on display in the shop are kept in locked cases. The reinforced glass is 200 times stronger than normal glass.

The Security Training Game Rules

- Every second, 6 people will be shown on-screen

- 5 will be guests
  1 will be a thief

- If you click on the thief, you gain 1 point

- If you click on a guest, you lose 2 points

- This happens 6 times in total

- **The aim of the game is to spot all 6 thieves and score 6 points**

In light of the theft, the owner <u>Viktor Volkov</u> has trained his security team to be on the alert for any customers behaving suspiciously. In the last year several petty crooks have been caught trying to unlock the display cases with <u>skeleton keys</u>.

The special exhibition Mr Volkov is hosting for the Monk Diamond will be the most high-profile event ever held by the <u>House of Volkov</u>. Mr Volkov decided to consult <u>Professor Bairstone</u> about the security strategy for the opening night of the exhibition.

The <u>Bond Brothers</u> have used disguises in past robberies and Mr Volkov and Professor Bairstone are worried that members of the gang, or their associates, might try to infiltrate the exhibition by posing as guests.

The agreed strategy is to use the method developed for <u>museums</u> in <u>London</u> by <u>Professor Li</u>. A <u>computer game</u> with a simple set of rules has proved to be an effective way of sharpening the <u>reaction times</u> of members of a security team.

The game needs to be built urgently so the team are properly trained before the opening of the special exhibition.

BUILDING A GAME

Now you've read the brief for Mission 5 you're ready to start building your game. This mission works in a slightly different way to the missions you have completed so far. You are going to build the game as you work through the mission. Follow the step-by-step instructions and copy the code and you'll have the game ready for Professor Bairstone in no time.

It's going to be a rush to get the game built in time, so start coding quickly!

1. Create a HTML file

Just like in all the other missions, the first thing we need to do is create a new HTML file. Call your new HTML file **securitygame.html**. Copy this code into your text-editing program:

Save your HTML file in your **Coding** folder on your desktop.

```
<!DOCTYPE html>
<html>
<head>
    <title>Security Game</title>
</head>
<body>
</body>
</html>
```

2. Build the game board

Now we need to build the basic structure of our game. We need to code a game board in our web page. The game board will be the area in our browser where the game will work. When the security team play the game, the guests and thief will appear on the game board.

Add your game board by coding an empty `<div>` in the `<body>` of your page. Add an id attribute to your `<div>`. Your `<body>` code will look like this:

```
<body>
  <div id="board">
  </div>
</body>
```

Id attribute

Then in your `<head>` add a CSS class that will change the look of your `<div>`. Use a CSS selector, called the id selector, to find your `<div>` by its id attribute. CSS selectors are an easy way to select various groups of elements to style. Using the CSS id selector is simple. All you have to do is create a class name using a hash (#) and the id attribute of the HTML element you want to change.

Create a CSS class called board that sets the CSS properties and values of your `<div>` to these things. The code for the CSS class in your `<head>` needs to look like this:

The game board needs:

- A 1px solid black border
- A grey background
- A height of 350px
- A width of 650px

```
<head>
    <title>Security Game</title>
    <style>
      #board {
        border: 1px solid black;
        background-color: gray;
        height: 350px;
        width: 650px;
      }
    </style>
</head>
```

CSS id selector

This is like the CSS element selector in Mission 1 or the CSS type attribute selector in Mission 3.

 Save your HTML file and open it in your browser. You will see your empty game board displayed on-screen.

Great work!

Security Ga

3. Add a button

Now we have a game board, we should add a button to our page. When the player clicks the button, the code for our game will run and the game will start.

Add your button above the `<div>` in your `<body>`. Create the button like you did in Mission 3, using the `<input/>` tag and type and value attributes. Set the onclick attribute of your `<input/>` tag to call a JavaScript function called startGame that will start the game. The code for your button will look like this:

```
<input type="button" value="Play" onclick="startGame()";/>
```

Now create the startGame function that your button will call when it's clicked. Add the function underneath the `<div>` in your `<body>`. Your `<script>` block will look like this:

```
<script>
  function startGame() {
  }
</script>
```

The complete code block in your text-editing program will now look like this:

You're becoming a real coding whiz!

```
<!DOCTYPE html>
<html>
<head>
  <title>Security Game</title>
  <style>
    #board {
      border: 1px solid black;
      background-color: gray;
      height: 350px;
      width: 650px;
    }
  </style>
</head>
<body>
  <input type="button" value="Play" onclick="startGame()";/>
  <div id="board">
  </div>
  <script>
    function startGame() {
    }
  </script>
</body>
</html>
```

Button

Function call

JavaScript function

158

Save your code and open it in your browser. You will see your button on-screen. At the moment when you click it, nothing will happen. We need to add some code to our startGame function.

Let's get that button working!

4. Create a JavaScript timer

Our game is going to test the reaction times of the security team at the House of Volkov. For our game to work, we need to learn how we can use JavaScript to run a piece of code again and again, after a certain period of time has passed. This is called a timer.

JavaScript has a built-in timer function called setTimeout, which allows you to call a function after a given amount of time has passed. All you have to do is give the setTimeout function the name of the function you want to call and the amount of time as arguments. As you know from Mission 2, you pass a function an argument by putting the argument in brackets. This time we are passing the function two arguments. Let's take a look at how you would use setTimeout to call a function after a certain time.

In this example the gameTimer function will be called after 1 second, or 1,000 milliseconds.

setTimeout function

Function to call

Amount of time to call it after

```
setTimeout(gameTimer, 1000);
```

Did you notice?

You have to use milliseconds with the setTimeout function. There are 1,000 milliseconds in a second. To work out the number of milliseconds you need, multiply the number of seconds by 1,000. So if you wanted your function to be called after 3 seconds, you would multiply 3 by 1,000.

Turn over to practise using the setTimeout function!

JavaScript timers, such as the setTimeout function, are very useful for building games. Let's have a go at using the setTimeout function, so you know how it works and can add it to your game later in the mission. Let's code a program that counts up a number every second.

1. Open up your text-editing program. Create a new HTML file called **timers.html**. Type out this code:

```
<!DOCTYPE html>
<html>
<head>
    <title>Timers</title>
</head>
<body>
    <div id="number">
    </div>
</body>
</html>
```

2. Now add the <script> tag to your <head>. Inside your <script> block create a variable and set its value to 0 using the assignment (=) operator, like this:

```
<head>
    <title>Timers</title>
    <script>
      var count = 0;
    </script>
</head>
```

3. Now create a function called updateCount. Every time the function is called it will use the addition operator (+) to add 1 to the value of your variable. Then use getElementById and innerHTML to find your empty <div> and set the contents to the variable. Your code will look like this:

```
<script>
  var count = 0;
  function updateCount() {
    count = count + 1;          Add 1        Update screen
    document.getElementById("number").innerHTML = count;
  }
</script>
                                    Find <div>
```

4. Now we need to add a function call to our `<body>`. Add the function call like this:

```
<body>
   <div id="number">
   </div>
     <script>
        updateCount();
     </script>
</body>
```

5. Finally we have to add a timer that will call our function every second to our `<script>` block. We need to use the setTimeout function. We have to pass the function name and the number of milliseconds to the setTimeout function as arguments. Our `<script>` block will look like this:

```
<script>
   var count = 0;
   function updateCount() {
      count = count + 1;
      document.getElementById("number").innerHTML = count;
      setTimeout(updateCount, 1000);
   }
</script>
```

Call updateCount in 1 second

 Save your HTML file and open it in your browser. You will see your timer in action. The setTimeout function will call your updateCount function every second. The function will run and every second 1 will be added to the value of your variable. The number in your browser will update automatically.

That's rather clever. I'm impressed!

How are we going to use this skill to build the game?

5. Create a game loop

Games are one of the most difficult things you can code and there are many different ways you can build them. A popular way is to use a game loop. You used a loop in Mission 3 and we are going to need to learn more about them to build our game.

A game loop is a JavaScript function that gets called over and over again while your game is running. You can use a game loop to check if a player has done something, draw a HTML element on your screen and run the code for the game.

We can use the setTimeout built-in function to create a game loop. We need to add a new function to our `<script>` block that pops up an alert every 3 seconds. Let's call this function gameLoop. This new function will be called when our button is clicked. Let's take a look at our code block:

```
<!DOCTYPE html>
<html>
<head>
    <title>Security Game</title>
    <style>
      #board {
        border: 1px solid black;
        background-color: gray;
        height: 350px;
        width: 650px;
      }
    </style>
</head>
<body>
    <input type="button" value="Play" onclick="startGame()";/>
    <div id="board">
    </div>
      <script>
        function startGame() {
            gameLoop();          Function call
        }
Function
        function gameLoop() {
            alert("Game over!");     Alert
            setTimeout(gameLoop, 3000);
        }             Timer
      </script>            Number of
</body>                    milliseconds
</html>
```

I wonder if I could sniff out the Bond Brothers? I've got a very good nose.

162

Once you have made these changes, save your code and open it in your browser. When you click your button and call your startGame function, the game loop will start to run. Your gameLoop function will be called every 3 seconds and every time an alert will pop up. Every time it pops up, press OK so it keeps popping up.

Play

Game over!

OK

Great start to the mission! But where's the thief?

6. Add the guests and thief to the game board

Now you've coded your game board, button and game loop, we need to add the characters to our game. We want six different characters to flash on-screen in different places every second. Five of the characters will be guests; one character will be a thief. The security team will test their reaction times by trying to click on the thief when he flashes on-screen.

Let's start creating the characters on our game board. Each character needs its own <div>. Create six <div> tags nested inside your game board <div> and number them 1 to 6, like this:

Let's get these characters coded!

```
<div id="board">
    <div>1</div>
    <div>2</div>
    <div>3</div>
    <div>4</div>
    <div>5</div>
    <div>6</div>
</div>
```

Save your code and refresh your page. You will see your six `<div>` tags on your game board, like this:

Now let's use CSS to change the design and layout of our `<div>` tags. Let's create a CSS class called character that will make our `<div>` tags square blue boxes. In your text-editing program, add this new CSS class to the `<style>` tag in your `<head>`. Your complete `<style>` block will now look like this:

```
<!DOCTYPE html>
<html>
<head>
  <title>Security Game</title>
  <style>
    #board {
      border: 1px solid black;
      background-color: gray;
      height: 350px;
      width: 650px;
    }
    .character {
      background-color: lightblue;
      width: 120px;
      height: 120px;
      padding: 10px;
      margin: 10px;
      float: left;
    }
  </style>
</head>
```

New CSS class

Did you notice?

We have used the float CSS property. This will make our `<div>` tags align with one another.

Then apply your new character CSS class to each of your six `<div>` tags using the class attribute, like you did in Mission 1. Your `<body>` will look like this:

```
<body>
  <input type="button" value="Play" onclick="startGame()";/>
  <div id="board">
    <div class="character">1</div>
    <div class="character">2</div>
    <div class="character">3</div>
    <div class="character">4</div>
    <div class="character">5</div>
    <div class="character">6</div>
  </div>
  <script>
    function startGame() {
      gameLoop();
    }
    function gameLoop() {
      alert("Game over!");
      setTimeout(gameLoop, 3000);
    }
  </script>
</body>
</html>
```

Class attribute

It's starting to look more like a game now!

Save your code and refresh your page. You will see the CSS properties applied to your `<div>` tags.

Something's making my nose itch.

Security Ga

| Play |

| 1 | 2 | 3 | 4 |
| 5 | 6 | | |

7. Use the game loop to stop the game

Now we've added our characters to the game board, we need to make some changes to our game loop. At the moment it pops up an alert every 3 seconds. We need to change our loop so it will stop after a certain period of time. We're going to do this by keeping count of how many times we loop. When our loop has run a certain number of times, our game will end.

To keep count of our loops, let's create a variable that will increase in value every time it's called. To do that we should code a variable called loops that is set to the value 0. Add this variable to your `<script>` block before your gameLoop function, like this:

```
<script>
  function startGame() {
    gameLoop();
  }
  var loops = 0;
  function gameLoop() {
    alert("Game over!");
    setTimeout(gameLoop, 3000);
  }
</script>
```

Variable

We need to use this variable in our gameLoop function. We want to add 1 to its value every time the function is called. To do this, we could code like this:

```
loops = loops + 1;
```

However we can actually use a new JavaScript operator to write the same instruction in a simpler and shorter way. It's called the increment operator (++) and it's just like the operators we learnt about in Mission 2. We can use the increment operator (++) to add 1 to the value of our variable. All we have to write is this:

Increment operator

```
loops++;
```

We can use the increment operator (++) in our gameLoop function to count how many times our loop has been called. Remove the alert from your gameLoop function and replace it with your new piece of code, like this:

```
function gameLoop() {
  loops++;
  setTimeout(gameLoop, 3000);
}
```

This gives me paws for thought!

166

5

Now we want to make sure that our game loops for a fixed number of times before the game ends. We do this by adding an if statement and an else statement to our gameLoop function, which will check how many times our loop has run.

We need to make sure that when the loop has run for a certain number of times, the setTimeout function calling the loop will stop and an alert will pop up. We want our loop to run 12 times. It will run every 3 seconds until the twelfth loop, when the game will end. Our game will last for a total of 33 seconds (11 multiplied by 3) before it ends on the twelfth loop. Let's have a look at our whole <script> block with the new variable, if statement and else statement:

```
<script>
  function startGame() {
    gameLoop();
  }
  var loops = 0;
  function gameLoop() {
    loops++;                            Timer
    if(loops < 12) {          If statement
      setTimeout(gameLoop, 3000);
    }
    else {                    Else
      alert("Game over!");    statement
    }
  }
</script>
```

The if statement checks how many times our loop has run. If it is less than (<) 12 times, it keeps running by calling setTimeout again. If it is more than 12 times, the else statement runs and an alert pops up.

Save your new code and refresh your page. Press the play button and wait until the alert pops up. Your game will now end after a certain period of time.

Don't forget you have to wait for 33 seconds before the alert will pop up!

8. Use CSS to show and hide the characters

During our game the guest and thief characters will flash up on-screen. The House of Volkov security team will have to spot and click on the thief before he disappears. We need to use CSS to make the characters appear and disappear as the game loop runs. To do this we have to learn a new CSS property that makes a HTML element appear or disappear from our browser. We can then use JavaScript to apply the property to our characters.

CSS property name	What does it do?	Example values
display	Changes how a HTML element appears on-screen	block; none;

The display CSS property has lots of different values. The two values we need for our game are "block" and "none". If you set the display property of a HTML element to none, the element will not appear on your screen. If you set the display property to block, the HTML element will display as a square.

In your text-editing program, add two new CSS classes called hidden and visible. Use the display property so your <style> block looks like this:

 Save your code.

```
<style>
  #board {
    border: 1px solid black;
    background-color: gray;
    height: 350px;
    width: 650px;
  }
  .character {
    background-color: lightblue;
    width: 120px;
    height: 120px;
    padding: 10px;
    margin: 10px;
    float: left;
  }
  .hidden {
    display: none;
  }
  .visible {
    display: block;
  }
</style>
```

Display CSS property

Let's have a quick go at using this new CSS property!

►USING THE DISPLAY CSS PROPERTY

Try using the CSS display property to make HTML elements appear and disappear on your screen. You'll need this to make your characters display correctly in your game.

1. Open up your text-editing program. Create a new HTML file called **display.html**. Type out the code below, then save your HTML file and open it in your browser. Your page will look like this:

```
<!DOCTYPE html>
<html>
<head>
   <title>Display</title>
</head>
<body>
   <div>Security</div>
   <div>Thief</div>
   <div>Guest</div>
</body>
</html>
```

2. Reopen your file in your text-editing program. Modify your second <div> by adding the display CSS property, so it looks like this:

```
<body>
   <div>Security</div>
   <div style="display: none;">Thief</div>
   <div>Guest</div>
</body>
```

3. Save your file and refresh your page. The display CSS property and none value will make your second <div> disappear from your screen.

Where did that element go?

9. Animate the characters

We now need to apply our two new CSS classes (hidden and visible) to our game loop so the character <div> tags become animated. To do this we need our game loop to add and remove the new CSS classes to and from our character <div> tags.

When our game runs, we want our characters to flash on and off the screen. We're currently looping around 12 times, so the character <div> tags need to be visible for 6 loops and invisible for 6 loops to create the flashing effect. The first thing we need is a new variable called peopleVisible to store this information. We need to set this variable to the value false, like this:

```
var peopleVisible = false
```

We need our variable to be set to false at the start so that the character <div> tags start off hidden on our screen. Then when the variable is set to true, the characters will appear on our screen.

When the game loop runs, we want the value stored in our new variable to alternate between true and false. To do this we have to use another JavaScript operator, called the not operator (!). You can use the not operator (!) to change the value of your variable.

Let's have a look at how we use the not operator (!) in our <script> block.

 Type these new pieces of code into your text-editing program and save your file.

```
<script>
  function startGame() {
    gameLoop();
  }
  var loops = 0;              Variable
  var peopleVisible = false;
  function gameLoop() {
    peopleVisible = !peopleVisible;
    loops++;              Not operator
    if(loops < 12) {
      setTimeout(gameLoop, 3000);
    }
    else {
      alert("Game over!");
    }
  }
</script>
```

We have used the not operator (!) to alternate the value of our new variable. If the value of our variable is false, when the variable runs in our gameLoop function the not operator (!) will change its value to true. And if the value of our variable is true, when the variable runs the not operator (!) will change its value to false.

Every time our loop runs, the loops variable will go up by one and the peopleVisible variable will alternate between true and false. As we loop round, our variables will look like this:

Now we need to add a new function called flashCharacters to our `<script>` block that will make our character `<div>` tags appear on-screen when the variable value is true. We do this using our two new CSS classes. When the value is true we want to use the visible CSS class, and when the value is false we want to use the hidden CSS class. Turn over to find out exactly how to code this flashCharacters function.

Loop number	Variable value
1	True
2	False
3	True
4	False
5	True
6	False
7	True
8	False
9	True
10	False
11	True
12	False
Game over	

I like using loops!

This new function sounds complicated!

10. Apply CSS using JavaScript

We need a new function that will apply a CSS class to the character `<div>` tags depending on the value of our variable. We should call this function flashCharacters. The function must find our game board, using getElementById, and store it in a variable called board. Then the function needs to pick a CSS class to apply to the character `<div>` tags. This will depend on the value of our peopleVisible variable.

To decide the CSS classes we create a second variable called classToSet that will store the two names of the CSS classes we need to set. We choose the CSS classes using an if and else statement. We set the value of our classToSet variable to an **empty string**. This empty string is filled as the if and else statements run. If our peopleVisible variable is true, our classToSet variable will be set to the visible CSS class. If our peopleVisible variable is false, the else statement will change our classToSet variable to the hidden CSS class.

We then need to code a loop which counts the 6 character `<div>` tags. As the loop counts the `<div>` tags it assigns the value of our classToSet variable to each `<div>`. We do this using the className method. The className method lets you set a CSS class on a HTML element in JavaScript.

Our complete function now looks like this:

```javascript
function flashCharacters() {
    var board = document.getElementById("board");
    var classToSet = "";
    if(peopleVisible) {
        classToSet = "character visible";
    }
    else {
        classToSet = "character hidden";
    }
    for(var index = 0; index < 6; index++) {
        board.children[index].className = classToSet;
    }
}
```

Variable
Variable
Empty string
Id attribute
If statement
CSS class name
CSS class name
Else statement
Loop
Class name method

Did you notice?

In the variable called index inside our loop we have stored more than one piece of information. This kind of variable is called a collection. We have to use square brackets ([ ]) to get a value out of the collection to use in our code.

CODE WORDS An **EMPTY STRING** is a piece of data, in the form of a sequence of characters, that has the value of 0. In JavaScript an empty string is represented as " ".

172

11. Simplify the conditional statements

This function looks quite complicated, so we should now try to simplify it. You can use another operator in JavaScript, called a conditional operator (?), to simplify the if and else statements. You use the conditional operator (?) like this:

Conditional operator

```
var variableName = condition ? value1 : value2;
```

This tells our browser that if the condition of our variable is true it should use value1, and if it is false use value2. So we can rewrite the code in our function like this:

Conditional operator   CSS class name   CSS class name

```
var classToSet = peopleVisible ? "character visible" : "character hidden";
```

Add your new flashCharacters function with the simplified if and else statements to your <script> block. Make sure your gameLoop function calls your new function too. Save your code and open it in your browser. Every 3 seconds your blue boxes will appear and disappear on your screen.

Turn over to see what our whole code block now looks like!

Get coding!

Don't forget you can view the code on the *Get Coding!* website too!

Check your code in your text-editing program. The code you need for your game will look like the block below. You have to refresh your page between each play of the game. Make any changes you need and save your file.

```html
<!DOCTYPE html>
<html>
<head>
  <title>Security Game</title>
  <style>
    #board {
      border: 1px solid black;
      background-color: gray;
      height: 350px;
      width: 650px;
    }
    .character {
      background-color: lightblue;
      width: 120px;
      height: 120px;
      padding: 10px;
      margin: 10px;
      float: left;
    }
    .hidden {
      display: none;
    }
    .visible {
      display: block;
    }
  </style>
</head>
```

```
<body>
  <input type="button" value="Play" onclick="startGame()";/>
  <div id="board">
    <div class="character">1</div>
    <div class="character">2</div>
    <div class="character">3</div>
    <div class="character">4</div>
    <div class="character">5</div>
    <div class="character">6</div>
  </div>
  <script>
    function startGame() {
      gameLoop();
    }
    var loops = 0;
    var peopleVisible = false;
    function gameLoop() {
      peopleVisible = !peopleVisible;
      flashCharacters();
      loops++;
      if(loops < 12) {
        setTimeout(gameLoop, 3000);
      }
      else {
        alert("Game over!");
      }
    }
    function flashCharacters() {
      var board = document.getElementById("board");
      var classToSet = peopleVisible ? "character visible" : "character hidden";
      for(var index = 0; index < 6; index++) {
        board.children[index].className = classToSet;
      }
    }
  </script>
</body>
</html>
```

But which characters are the guests and which is the thief?

Function call

Simplified if statement

Turn over to create the characters!

12. create the thief

At the moment in our game, every 3 seconds our characters flash on and off the screen. What we need to do now is change the position of our characters on-screen every time our game loop runs. Every 3 seconds the characters need to move to a different place on the game board. And we need to make one of the characters the thief.

We first need to add a function that creates a new set of characters, in different positions, every time our game loop runs. Let's call this function createCharacters. Start by adding the function call in your gameLoop function, like this:

```
function gameLoop() {
   peopleVisible = !peopleVisible;
   createCharacters();
   flashCharacters();
   loops++;
   if(loops < 12) {
      setTimeout(gameLoop, 3000);
   }
   else {
      alert("Game over!");
   }
}
```

Function call

Then code the new createCharacters function before your flashCharacters function:

```
function createCharacters() {
   var board = document.getElementById("board");
   for(var index = 0; index < 6; index ++) {
      board.children[index].innerHTML = "Guest";
   }
}
```

This is very similar to the function we coded earlier to set the CSS class of each character `<div>`. But this time we've used innerHTML, like we used in Mission 3, to set the value of each of the characters to "Guest".

 Save your HTML file and refresh your page. Now when you press *Play*, you'll see that each of the character `<div>` tags is labelled "Guest".

Now we need to add some code to our createCharacters function that will randomly pick one of the 6 character `<div>` tags to be the thief, every time the game loop runs. We need to write code that will pick a random number. There isn't an easy way of picking a random number using JavaScript, so the next piece of code you need is quite complicated. Carefully type this new code at the end of your createCharacters function, so that it looks like this:

```
function createCharacters() {
    var board = document.getElementById("board");
    for(var index = 0; index < 6; index ++) {
        board.children[index].innerHTML = "Guest";
    }
    var randomNumber = Math.floor(Math.random() * 6) + 1;
    board.children[randomNumber-1].innerHTML = "Thief";
}
```

Math API

Here we are using a new API called the Math API. It works in exactly the same way as the DOM and localStorage APIs that we used in Mission 3. Using the Math API lets you access handy maths functions that have been built in to your web browser. To find a random number you have to do the following calculation:

```
Math.floor(Math.random() * BIGGEST_NUMBER) + SMALLEST_NUMBER;
```

We have 6 characters in our game, so our biggest number is 6 and our smallest number is 1. We need to code:

```
Math.floor(Math.random() * 6) + 1;
```

We must get the diamond back!

We then store the result of our calculation in a variable. Then we can use this variable in our next line of code. We use innerHTML to set the value of whichever `<div>` matches our random number, like this:

```
board.children[randomNumber-1].innerHTML = "Thief"
```

Because our numbers in JavaScript count up from 0, we're going to subtract 1 from our random number, so we'll only ever get the numbers 0, 1, 2, 3, 4 and 5.

 Save your code. Your new createCharacter function will have added a thief to your game. Now when you press *Play*, every time your game loop runs a random character on your game board will become the thief.

13. create a score

Now we have a game board that shows us a different set of characters every 3 seconds. One of those characters is the thief that the House of Volkov's security team need to catch. What we need to do now is create a way for the user to click on the thief. When the user clicks, they catch the thief and score a point.

We first have to add a variable called gameScore, to keep track of the score. It goes underneath the startGame function at the top of our <script> block:

```
var loops = 0;
var peopleVisible = false;
var gameScore = 0;
```

Every time the player clicks on the thief, we need to add 1 point to their score. And to make sure the player is paying attention, every time they click on a guest we should take away 2 points. To create our scoring system we need to add an onclick to every character, every time our game loop runs. Add this new code to your createCharacter function:

```
function createCharacters() {
    var board = document.getElementById("board");
    for(var index = 0; index < 6; index ++) {
        board.children[index].innerHTML = "Guest";
        board.children[index].onclick = function() {
            gameScore += -2;
        }
    }
    var randomNumber = Math.floor(Math.random() * 6) + 1;
    board.children[randomNumber-1].innerHTML = "Thief";
    board.children[randomNumber-1].onclick = function() {
        gameScore++;
    }
}
```

Variable · Operator · Onclick · Variable · Operator · Onclick

We're using the onclick just like we did in Mission 3. When a guest or thief is created, an onclick is added. We're using two new arithmetic operators to change the value of our gameScore variable. If the user clicks on a guest, the += operator means the value that follows is added to the value in the variable. In this case, since the value that follows is –2, it means that 2 is subtracted from the gameScore value. If the user clicks on a thief, the increment operator (++) means 1 is added to the value in the variable.

We also need to change the alert message when the game ends, so that it tells the user their score. Change the else statement in your gameLoop function so it uses the gameScore variable value, like this:

```
function gameLoop() {
  peopleVisible = !peopleVisible;
  createCharacters();
  flashCharacters();
  loops++;
  if(loops < 12) {
    setTimeout(gameLoop, 3000);
  }
  else {
    alert("You scored " + gameScore);
  }
}
```

Variable

Did you notice?

We leave a space at the end of our alert text, so the message displays correctly with the gameScore value.

Save your HTML file and refresh your page. Try clicking on the thief every time it flashes on-screen. See how many points you score at the end of the game. Remember you need to refresh your page between each play of the game.

Hurray! The diamond will surely be safe now!

14. Simplify the code

Our game now works and the House of Volkov's security team can soon begin their training. But you might have noticed that our createCharacters and flashCharacters functions are quite similar. One creates our characters and the other adds a CSS

class to them. We can now combine these functions to make our code simpler. Simplifying your code as you work through a problem is a really common thing to do when you're coding. It makes it much easier to understand your code.

We should change our createCharacters function so it adds the CSS class as well as creating the characters. Change the function so it looks like this:

```
function createCharacters() {
    var board = document.getElementById("board");
    var classToSet = peopleVisible ? "character visible" : "character hidden";
    for(var index = 0; index < 6; index ++) {
        board.children[index].className = classToSet;
        board.children[index].innerHTML = "Guest";
        board.children[index].onclick = function() {
            gameScore += -2;
        }
    }
    var randomNumber = Math.floor(Math.random() * 6) + 1;
    board.children[randomNumber-1].innerHTML = "Thief";
    board.children[randomNumber-1].onclick = function() {
        gameScore++;
    }
}
```

CSS classes added

This function now does everything. Every time the game loop runs, it picks up the correct CSS class, creates the characters and then sets the onclick for each character. We no longer need the flashCharacters function, so we can delete it. Also delete the function call from your gameLoop function so it looks like this:

```
function gameLoop() {
    peopleVisible = !peopleVisible;
    createCharacters();
    loops++;
    if(loops < 12) {
        setTimeout(gameLoop, 3000);
    }
    else {
        alert("You scored " + gameScore);
    }
}
```

Function call for flashCharacters removed

Save your code.
Your game will work in exactly the same way.

Smart coding, my friend!

5

15. Designing the game with CSS

We've got the basic structure of our game working now, but it doesn't look very fun on-screen. Let's use our CSS skills from Mission 1 to design it. First let's see if we can make our thief look more distinctive when he flashes up on-screen. Let's add a new CSS class called thief to our <style> block, like this:

```css
.character {
    background-color: lightblue;
    width: 120px;
    height: 120px;
    padding: 10px;
    margin: 10px;
    float: left;
}
.thief {
    background-color: red;
}
```

Then we need to apply this CSS class to our JavaScript. Every time the thief is added we need to add this new CSS class. To do that we need to make this change to our code:

```javascript
var randomNumber = Math.floor(Math.random() * 6) + 1;
board.children[randomNumber-1].innerHTML = "Thief";
board.children[randomNumber-1].onclick = function() {
    gameScore++;
}
board.children[randomNumber-1].className = classToSet + " thief";
```

Every time our game loop runs, this will apply our thief CSS class to our thief <div> and make it red. Save your HTML file. Your thief will now be different to the guest.

Did you notice?

There is a space in the code " thief ". This space is essential because we are using two CSS class names: the CSS class we've picked using our classToSet variable (hidden or visible), and the CSS class thief. We need the space so it doesn't end up as "hiddenthief".

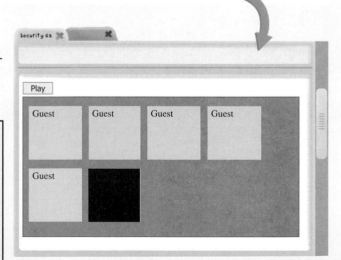

16. Use images for the characters

If we want to make our character `<div>` tags look a bit more exciting, we're going to have to learn some new CSS properties. The new properties are very simple and work in exactly the same way as the ones you learnt in Mission 1.

First of all, go to the *Get Coding!* website and find these two images:

Save these images with all your other HTML files in your **Coding** folder on your desktop. You've done this before in Mission 1, so go back to pages 28–30 if you need a reminder.

Guest

Thief

Now we're going to change the CSS classes in our `<style>` block. We're going to use two new CSS properties: the background and background-size CSS properties.

CSS property	What does it do?	Example values
background	Sets the background of a HTML element to an image	url('image.jpg'); none;
background-size	Sets the size of the background image in a HTML element	cover; 650px;

We can use these two new CSS properties in our character and thief CSS classes, like this:

```css
.character {
    background: url('guest.jpg');
    background-size: cover;
    width: 120px;
    height: 120px;
    padding: 10px;
    margin: 10px;
    float: left;
}
.thief {
    background: url('thief.jpg');
    background-size: cover;
}
```

Background property

Background-size property

That thief's got an ugly mug!

Using the background CSS property, we ask our browser to use saved images as the background for our <div> tags. Then using the background-size CSS property, we ask our browser to make sure that the image file is set to a big enough size to cover the whole background of each <div>.

 Save your HTML file and see what the new CSS properties have done to your game.

Now we have the images set as the background of the character <div> tags, let's remove the guest and thief labels. After all, we don't want it to be too easy for the House of Volkov's security team. Remove the text by changing these two lines in your <script> block:

```
board.children[index].innerHTML = "Guest";

board.children[randomNumber-1].innerHTML = "Thief";
```

Change them to empty strings, like this:

```
board.children[index].innerHTML = "";

board.children[randomNumber-1].innerHTML = "";
```

The game is looking great!

 Save your HTML file. Now your game will just be made up of pictures.

I don't like the look of that thief.

17. change the game board

Now we know how to use the background and background-size CSS properties, we can easily change our game board from the grey colour to an image. Go to the *Get Coding!* website and find the background image. Save it in your **Coding** folder.

All we then have to do is add the new background and background-size properties to the board CSS class in our `<style>` block. Don't forget to delete the background-color CSS class, as it is no longer needed.
Your code will look like this:

We should also make sure that at the start of the game, when it loads in our browser, we just see the game board. Then when we press play, we see the characters. To do this we need to add the CSS display property to the character CSS class in our `<style>` block, like this:

Save your HTML file. When your game loads, you will see the new background for your game board. When you press *Play* your characters will load on-screen and your game will begin.

```css
#board {
  background: url('background.jpg');
  background-size: cover;
  border: 1px solid black;
  height: 350px;
  width: 650px;
}


.character {
  background: url('guest.jpg');
  background-size: cover;
  width: 120px;
  height: 120px;
  padding: 10px;
  margin: 10px;
  float: left;
  display: none;
}
```

Start Screen

Game Screen

184

18. Make the game harder

You might have noticed that the 3 second delay makes it easy to click on the thief. We now need to make the game harder so it's more of a challenge. The characters need to flash on-screen for a much shorter time so there will be less time to click on the thief. To do this we need to change the setTimeout call, like this:

```
setTimeout(gameLoop, peopleVisible ? 1000 : 3000);
```

We're using a simplified if statement, like we did earlier in the mission. We've changed our setTimeout call so that if peopleVisible is true, our gameLoop function will be called in 1 second. If peopleVisible is false, our gameLoop function will be called in 3 seconds. So now our characters will only flash on-screen for 1 second, but when they're invisible they will be hidden for 3 seconds.

Save your code and start playing your finished game. Can you score 6 points?

DO IT YOURSELF TASK
YOUR FINISHED GAME

Coding a game is challenging and you've mastered it in this mission. Professor Bairstone will be delighted. The game will test the security team's reaction times.

Security Training Game Brief

Check that you have correctly coded all the things below in your **securitygame.html** file and that it's saved in your **Coding** folder. Don't forget you can change the speed of your game, making it faster and even harder for the user.

- ♥ A game board
- ♥ 5 guests
- ♥ 1 thief
- ♥ A play button
- ♥ A score alert

Turn over to see the full code block for the game.

```
<!DOCTYPE html>
<html>
<head>
  <title>Security Game</title>
  <style>
    #board {
      background: url('background.jpg');
      background-size: cover;
      border: 1px solid black;
      height: 350px;
      width: 650px;
    }
    .character {
      background: url('guest.jpg');
      background-size: cover;
      width: 120px;
      height: 120px;
      padding: 10px;
      margin: 10px;
      float: left;
      display: none;
    }
    .thief {
      background: url('thief.jpg');
      background-size: cover;
    }
    .hidden {
      display: none;
    }
    .visible {
      display: block;
    }
  </style>
</head>
<body>
  <input type="button" value="Play" onclick="startGame()";/>
  <div id="board">
    <div class="character">1</div>
    <div class="character">2</div>
    <div class="character">3</div>
    <div class="character">4</div>
```

Mission 5 completed! Amazing work!

```
      <div class="character">5</div>
      <div class="character">6</div>
    </div>
    <script>
      function startGame() {
        gameLoop();
      }
      var loops = 0;
      var peopleVisible = false;
      var gameScore = 0;
      function gameLoop() {
        peopleVisible = !peopleVisible;
        createCharacters();
        loops++;
        if(loops < 12) {
          setTimeout(gameLoop, peopleVisible ? 1000 : 3000);
        }
        else {
          alert("You scored " + gameScore);
        }
      }
      function createCharacters() {
        var board = document.getElementById("board");
        var classToSet = peopleVisible ? "character visible" : "character hidden";
        for(var index = 0; index < 6; index ++) {
          board.children[index].className = classToSet;
          board.children[index].innerHTML = "";
          board.children[index].onclick = function() {
            gameScore += -2;
          }
        }
        var randomNumber = Math.floor(Math.random() * 6) + 1;
        board.children[randomNumber-1].innerHTML = "";
        board.children[randomNumber-1].onclick = function() {
            gameScore++;
        }
        board.children[randomNumber-1].className = classToSet + " thief";
      }
    </script>
  </body>
</html>
```

FUTURE CODE SKILLS

This mission was an important step in learning about JavaScript game programming. You used a game loop, an essential part of nearly all computer games, to power your game and create an interactive experience for the user. This isn't an easy thing to do, so well done! You can now use your knowledge about game loops to build more complicated games that will respond to your user in different ways.

Mission 6

YOUR FINISHED WEBSITE

- ◆ LEARN HOW TO USE WIREFRAMES

- ◆ BUILD A WEBSITE USING HTML AND CSS

- ◆ LINK YOUR WEB PAGES TOGETHER

- ◆ MAKE YOUR WEBSITE LIVE

Mission Brief

Dear Coder,

We think you'll be pleased to hear that the special exhibition at the House of Volkov was a resounding success! We want to thank you for all your help and hard work. When Mr Volkov unveiled the Monk Diamond to the guests everyone was amazed. It was the proudest moment of our careers.

The evening was not without drama though. As we feared, the Bond Brothers had found out about the diamond. They disguised themselves as guests and used false invitations to gain access to the exhibition. Luckily, once they got inside a member of the security team immediately noticed that they were behaving suspiciously near the diamond's glass case. Mr Volkov intervened and the police were called just in time. Thanks to you, the Bond Brothers are now behind bars.

The news about the Monk Diamond has spread quickly and caused quite a stir, both in Moscow and around the world. Mr Volkov is so delighted to have it back in its rightful home, he wants to open the special exhibition to the public. Now we know the security team is up to the challenge, we think it'll be a jolly good show. And if people in Moscow like the exhibition, Mr Volkov is thinking about taking it on a tour around the world. The House of Volkov has a very exciting future ahead.

There's only one thing left to do and we thought you would like to help. Mr Volkov needs to build a whole website (not just a web page) that will tell everyone, all over the world, about the exhibition. We hope we can rely on you one last time! Who knows, perhaps you'll be able to come and see the Monk Diamond one day? We'd love to meet you and thank you in person.

Warmest celebratory wishes from the House of Volkov,
Professor Harry Bairstone, Dr Ruby Day and Ernest

PS Attached is Professor Bairstone's latest entry on the Explorer's Encyclopedia and a note from Mr Volkov.

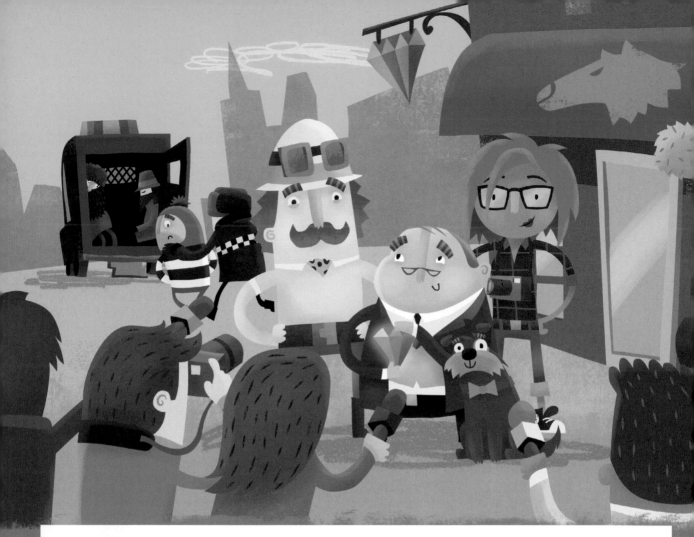

The Discovery of the Monk Diamond

From the Explorer's Encyclopedia, the guide to every adventure

This entry is about the discovery of the stolen jewel. For the entry about the diamond's history, see here.

The **Discovery of the Monk Diamond** was the discovery of the stolen Monk Diamond, made by Professor Bairstone and Dr Day in Siberia. Professor Bairstone had long believed that the Bond Brothers were responsible for the theft and that they had hidden the jewel far away from the House of Volkov in Moscow, where it was stolen.

VIKTOR VOLKOV
The House of Volkov, near to St Basil's Cathedral, Moscow

Dear Coder,

I just wanted to write you a short note to say thank you so much for all you have done to bring the Monk Diamond back to the House of Volkov. I was heartbroken when it was stolen and in my darker moments I thought I would have to sell the business. The House of Volkov has been run by my family for generations and it would have been devastating. But thanks to you, Professor Bairstone, Dr Day and Ernest, the Monk Diamond has been returned. I am so delighted to be hosting the exhibition and have the jewel on display in the shop.

As you know, a reward was offered for its safe return or the capture of the Bond Brothers. Professor Bairstone and Dr Day have taken their share and are going to use it to fund another expedition together. I want you to know that I also have a token of gratitude to give to you. It will be waiting for you when you come to Moscow to see the Monk Diamond for yourself.

With very warm and kind regards,
Viktor Volkov

Professor Bairstone is an explorer, known for discovering ancient artefacts around the world. He is always accompanied on his expeditions by Ernest, his dog. Before finding the Monk Diamond, his most notable discovery was the Hoy Hoard of Viking treasure, which he unearthed on the Orkney Islands in Scotland.

Dr Day is a scientist who studies fossils. She is currently researching a new species of feathered dinosaur. She has been on several different expeditions in the hope of discovering fossils to prove that this species had feathers.

The news that the Monk Diamond had been found in Siberia and returned to the House of Volkov made headlines all over the world. The team were interviewed for lots of different TV stations and have featured in many newspapers and magazines. Professor Bairstone has been invited to give lectures about the discovery and his biography will be published next year. Dr Day has been made a senior fellow at her university.

The special exhibition at the House of Volkov has been very popular. Mr Volkov told reporters he was "delighted by the return of the diamond and the success of the exhibition". Queues of up to two hours were reported outside the House of Volkov and sales of jewellery have more than doubled.

BUILD A WEBSITE

You've done some great work in the last five missions. You can now code using HTML, CSS and JavaScript and know how to use APIs to build more complex programs. You've built a web page, created a password, built a web-based app, planned a route and built a game. Now there is one final challenge: to build a website.

So far all the pages and programs you've built have been stored in your computer's web browser and have only been for Professor Bairstone and Dr Day to use. What we need to do now is learn how to build a website that can be accessed by anyone, anywhere in the world.

Building a website is not that different from building a web page, as we did in Mission 1. After all, a website is just a group of connected web pages. In this mission we are going to work in a slightly different way though. This time we are going to build our web pages using a tool called a wireframe. There will be five wireframes in this mission, and you will code a web page from each one.

Wireframes

Wireframes are a useful way of planning the content and layout of a website before you start coding. A wireframe is just a very simple drawing, like the example on the right, that shows the different elements of your page. They help you plan out the design of each web page and make important decisions about how a page will be structured.

Wireframes also help you decide how your user will interact with the page and move between the other pages on the website. Once you are happy with your wireframe you can then start coding, using it as a plan that shows you exactly what needs coding where on your page.

In this mission we are going to code a website made up of five web pages. Each of the five pages will link together and tell a different part of the diamond's exciting story. We are going to look at a possible wireframe for each page of the Monk Diamond website.

Menu bar

A big image

Wireframe

Home / Discovery / Exhibition / The House of Volkov

The Monk Diamond is one of the rarest and most valuable diamonds in Europe. It has a fascinating history. It was owned by Russian nobility, stolen by a famous criminal gang and then found hidden in remote mountains in one of the most sensational discoveries of the century. Find out more about the Monk Diamond in this website or come and see it for yourself at the House of Volkov in Moscow.

Contact Professor Bairstone: profbairstone@intrepidexplorer.com

Text

Footer

Image

6

Let's take a look at the five web pages we're going to code to make the Monk Diamond website:

Web page	Content
index.html	Our home page, explaining about the discovery and exhibition
diamond.html	The history of the Monk Diamond, including the theft
discovery.html	The story of Professor Bairstone and Dr Day's discovery
exhibition.html	The details of the exhibition, including opening times
volkov.html	How to get to the House of Volkov in Moscow

As we work through this mission, we'll look at a wireframe for each page of our website. You can then code each web page in your text-editing program using the HTML, CSS and JavaScript skills you've learnt in all the other missions.

MORE CSS PROPERTIES

In Mission 1 you learnt that CSS is a programming language that lets you change the look of a HTML web page. Before we start looking at wireframes, we need to learn about a few more CSS properties and values.

Using images

When you add images to your pages, you can change the size of them in lots of different ways. The best way to do it is to add a style attribute to your `<img/>` tag and set the width CSS property to a value in pixels (px) or a percentage (%), like this:

Style attribute   Pixels

```
<img src="diamond.jpg" alt="The Jewel" style="width: 150px"/>
```

```
<img src="ernest.jpg" alt="Dog" style="height: 50%"/>
```

Percentage

Your browser will then automatically work out what height your image should be. If you want to stretch an image out and stop it being in proportion, you can use both the width and height CSS properties in your style attribute, like this:

Width property   Height property

```
<img src="profB.jpg" alt="Explorer" style="width: 50px; height: 50px"/>
```

Making an image fill a <div>

A good way to create an interesting layout is to use <div> tags to divide your page into different sections. If you want to use an image as the background for a <div> and create a banner, you should use the background and background-size CSS properties like you did in Mission 5. There are different ways to **scale** your images using CSS properties.

CSS property	What does it do?	Example values
background	Sets the background image for a HTML element	url(filename.jpg);
background-size	Sets the size of the background of a HTML element	contain; cover; auto;

In Mission 5 you used the cover value with the background-size CSS property. The cover value scales the background image so it is big enough to completely fill your <div>. Some of the image might be **cropped** to make it fit the size of the <div>.

As well as the cover value, you can also use the contain value. The contain value makes the background image as big as possible without stretching it out of shape. Depending on the size of your image, it might not fill your whole <div>. If the image doesn't fill the space, your browser will repeat it.

If you use auto as the value for the background-size CSS property, it will also repeat the image as many times as it needs to fill up the <div>.

```
<style>
  .team {
    width: 600px;
    height: 600px;
    background: url(team.jpg);
    background-size: contain;
  }
</style>
```
Contain value

CODE WORDS When we **SCALE** an image we resize it by making it bigger, smaller or giving it different proportions. When we **CROP** an image we cut its edges off, making the image smaller.

Aligning text and images

You can make images and text line up in two simple ways, which we looked at in Mission 1. You can use the text-align CSS property on the `<div>` that has the text and image inside it. Or you can use the float CSS property in a style attribute inside your `<img/>` tag, like this:

Float property

```
<img src="team.jpg" alt="The Team" style="float: right;"/>
```

More CSS colour values

So far you have been using colour names as the values for your CSS colour properties. By default, your browser supports about 140 colour names. In addition to these names, you can create your own colours using a HEX code. You use a HEX code in exactly the same way as you use a colour name. They look like this:

HEX code

```
<body>
  <div style="background-color: #0BFF54;">
     Professor Bairstone, Dr Day and Ernest were on the expedition.
  </div>
</body>
```

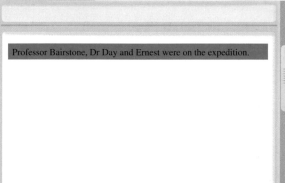

Luckily you don't need to remember HEX codes. There are plenty of websites that help you work them out. You can mix your own colours and make your own HEX codes using the Colour Wheel at **www.color.adobe.com**. Just copy the HEX value from the page into your code and remember to start your HEX code colour with a hash (#).

I can't wait to see your finished website!

195

1. The home page: index.html

The home page (**index.html**) is the most important page of your website because it's the page your user will see first. A good home page will make the purpose of the website obvious and engage the user's interest. It should be clear that it is only a home page and that there are other web pages on the site for the user to discover.

On our home page, let's use a big image of the Monk Diamond as the header banner for our page.

We can put a title in the banner too. Then let's have a menu bar that contains links to all the other pages on our site. Then we should have a short piece of text that explains a little bit about the Monk Diamond's discovery. Underneath the text let's have a button that links to the House of Volkov page on the website. Finally, we can have a footer with contact details for Professor Bairstone. Let's take a look at a wireframe of this page:

Home

Header banner

The Monk Diamond
An extraordinary exhibition

Title

Menu bar

The Diamond / Discovery / Exhibition / The House of Volkov

The Monk Diamond is one of the rarest and most valuable diamonds in Europe. It has a fascinating history. It was owned by Russian nobility, stolen by a famous criminal gang and then found hidden in remote mountains in one of the most sensational discoveries of the century. Find out more about the Monk Diamond in this website or come and see it for yourself at the House of Volkov in Moscow.

Text

Button

Visit the House of Volkov

Contact Professor Bairstone: profbairstone@intrepidexplorer.com

Footer

My email address is profbairstone@intrepidexplorer.com

Code this page using the HTML and CSS skills you've mastered in earlier missions.

Find images of the Monk Diamond on the *Get Coding!* website.

Header banner

- In your `<style>` block, create a CSS class with the width property set to 100%, the height set to 400px and the padding set to 0px. Use the background and background-size CSS properties to add an image.
- Apply this CSS class to a `<div>` in the `<body>` of your page.
- Add title text to your `<div>`. Use a style attribute to change the font-size and color CSS properties.

Menu bar

- Create a second `<div>` in the `<body>` of your page. Add a style attribute to your `<div>` tag and set the width, padding and background-color CSS properties.
- Add four hyperlinks, using the anchor `<a>` tag and href attribute.
- You could also create a `<div>` for each link and set them to float to the right of each other.

Text

- Create a third `<div>`, using the style attribute to set the width to 100% and the padding to 50px.
- Add your text, using the `<p>` and `<br/>` tags to divide the text into sections.

Button

- Create a button by putting a link inside a `<div>`. Use a style attribute with the width, height, padding and background-color CSS properties to make it look like a button.

Footer

- Create a final `<div>` and use the style attribute to set the width to 100%.
- Add text inside the `<div>` with contact information for Professor Bairstone.

You can find the code for this wireframe and all the others in the mission on the *Get Coding!* website.

When you've finished coding your page, save your HTML file in your **Coding** folder. Call your file **index.html**.

2. The diamond page: diamond.html

The diamond page (**diamond.html**) is the second web page in our website and will tell the user all about the fascinating history of the Monk Diamond. Let's take a look at the wireframe we need to build this page:

Menu bar
- Create a `<div>` in the `<body>` of your page. Add a style attribute to your `<div>` tag and set the width, padding and background-color CSS properties. Add four hyperlinks, using the anchor `<a>` tag and href attribute.
- You could also create a `<div>` for each link and set them to float to the right of each other.

Big image
- In your `<style>` block, create a CSS class with the width property set to 100%, the height set to 200px and the padding set to 0px. Use the background and background-size CSS properties to add an image. Apply this CSS class to a second `<div>` in the `<body>`.

Text
- Create a third `<div>`, using the style attribute to set the width to 100% and the padding to 50px. Add your text, using the `<p>` and `<br/>` tags to divide the text into sections.

Image
- Add an image inside your text `<div>`. Use the style attribute with the width, height and text-align CSS properties to centre it.

Footer
- Make this the same as the home page.

Menu bar

Big image

The Diamond

Home / Discovery / Exhibition / The House of Volkov

The Monk Diamond is famous for its distinctive green colour. A Russian nobleman bought the diamond for his wife in 1889, but it was stolen during the Russian Revolution. For the next 30 years, the Monk Diamond's whereabouts were unknown. In 1947 it was discovered during a police raid on a gang of petty criminals in Moscow. It was returned to the nobleman's family. The nobleman's son decided the Monk Diamond was unlucky and sold it to the House of Volkov, Moscow's oldest jewellery house. The House of Volkov paid an undisclosed sum for the jewel, but it was rumoured to be the most expensive diamond sale ever.

Contact Professor Bairstone: profbairstone@intrepidexplorer.com

Text

Image

Footer

When you've finished coding your page, save your HTML file in your **Coding** folder. Call your file **diamond.html**.

3. The discovery page: discovery.html

The discovery page (**discovery.html**) is the third page and will tell the user how Professor Bairstone and Dr Day found the Monk Diamond. Let's create a wireframe with a slightly different layout to our previous page, like this:

Menu bar
◆ This should be the same as the menu bar on the diamond page. Remember to update the links.

Big image
◆ In your `<style>` block, create a CSS class with the width property set to 100%, the height set to 200px and the padding set to 0px. Use the background and background-size CSS properties to add an image. Apply this CSS class to a second `<div>` in the `<body>`.

Text column
◆ Create a `<div>`, using the style attribute to set the width to 80% and the padding to 50px. Add your text, using the `<p>` and `<br/>` tags to divide the text into sections.

Image column
◆ Create another `<div>` and use the style attribute to set the width CSS property to 20%. Float this `<div>` to the right of the `<div>` with your text in.
◆ Add an image inside your `<div>`. Use the style attribute with the width, height and text-align CSS properties to centre it.

Footer
◆ Make this the same as the home page.

 When you've finished coding your page, save your HTML file in your **Coding** folder. Call your file **discovery.html**.

4. The exhibition page: exhibition.html

The exhibition page (**exhibition.html**) will have all the details about the exhibition at the House of Volkov. As it contains important information, we want to keep the layout simple so the information is easy to see and understand. Let's take a look at the wireframe:

Menu bar
- This should be the same as the menu bar on the diamond and discovery pages. Just remember to update the links.

Big image
- This should also be the same as the diamond and discovery pages.

Text
- Create a `<div>` for each section of information.
- You can indent pieces of text using the style attribute and setting the CSS margin property to 10px.

Footer
- Make this the same as the home page.

Menu bar

Big image

Exhibition

Home / The Diamond / Discovery / The House of Volkov

The Special Exhibition

The House of Volkov
Opening times
Monday to Friday
  9.30–6.00
    Last admission 5.30
Saturdays and Sundays
  11.00–4.00
    Last admission 3.30
Admission: Free
Please note cameras are not allowed inside the House of Volkov.

Contact Professor Bairstone: profbairstone@intrepidexplorer.com

Text

Footer

Using `<div>` tags to create different layouts works really well!

When you've finished coding your page, save your HTML file in your **Coding** folder. Call your file **exhibition.html**.

5. The House of Volkov page: volkov.html

For the final page of our website (**volkov.html**) we need to give directions to the House of Volkov, so people know where to find it. We should give the address and also embed a map from Google, using the Google Maps Embed API like we did in Mission 4. Let's take a look at the wireframe:

Menu bar

- This should be the same as the menu bar on the diamond, discovery and exhibition pages. Just remember to update the links.

Big image

- This should also be the same as the diamond, discovery and exhibition pages.

Text column

- Create a `<div>`, using the style attribute to set the width to 80% and the padding to 50px. Add your text using the `<p>` and `<br/>` tags to divide the text into sections.

Map column

- Create another `<div>` and use the style attribute to set the width CSS property to 20%. Float this `<div>` to the right of the `<div>` with your text in.
- Add an `<iframe>` and set the width, height and border attributes. Then add a source attribute with a URL that links to the Google Maps Embed API. Use the search API function and embed a map showing St Basil's Cathedral in Moscow.

Footer

- Make this the same as the home page.

Menu bar

Big image

The House of ✖

Home / The Diamond / Discovery / Exhibition

The House of Volkov

The House of Volkov is the oldest jewellery house in Moscow.
Please come and visit us.
We are near to St Basil's Cathedral.
   Address:
   The House of Volkov
   St Basil's Cathedral
   Moscow

Contact Professor Bairstone: profbairstone@intrepidexplorer.com

Text column

Footer

Map column

 When you've finished coding your page, save your HTML file in your **Coding** folder. Call your file **volkov.html**.

YOUR FINISHED WEBSITE

Now you've built your five web pages, the final thing you need to do is check that all your links are correct and your pages connect in the way that you had planned. Check the menu bar on each of your web pages has the correct file names in each of the links. If your links aren't right your website won't work, as the user won't be able to navigate between the pages. Your code for each link will look like this:

```
<a href="index.html">Home</a>
<a href="diamond.html">The Diamond</a>
<a href="discovery.html">Discovery</a>
<a href="exhibition.html">Exhibition</a>
<a href="volkov.html">The House of Volkov</a>
```

Making your own wireframes

Making your own wireframes is very easy. Lots of people just use a pencil, piece of paper and sticky notes to do it, drawing a wireframe that shows what their website will look like before they start to code. This is sometimes called paper **prototyping**. It's a really quick way to experiment with your layouts before you spend time coding them up.

If you want to make wireframes like the ones we've used here, there are plenty of tools available. You can use Microsoft Visio on a PC, Gliffy and Balsamiq mock-ups in a web browser, or OmniGraffle if you're on a Mac. All these programs come with pre-made graphics that you can use to quickly sketch out your pages on a computer.

CODE WORDS A **PROTOTYPE** is the first version of an object. The prototype is used to see what needs to be changed and improved in later versions and the finished object.

That's the final mission accomplished!

202

Making your website live

If you want other people to see your finished website, you need to upload it to a web server. At the start of the book we learnt about web servers. They can be hardware or software and they store websites so your web browser can access them. For people to be able to see your website, you need to **host** it on a web server on the Internet. Setting up your own web server is complicated, so luckily there are lots of online companies that will let you use their servers to host your files.

CODE WORDS When a web server stores a website so web browsers can access it we say the server **HOSTS** the website. When files are hosted by a server, they'll have a URL (web address) just like all the other websites on the Internet.

If you want to find a free web server to host your website, you will be able to find lots to choose from on the Internet. Just search for "free web hosting". Sometimes home Internet connections come with web space that you can use. Once you have a web host, you'll have to copy your files to their server. Carefully read the instructions and terms and conditions that your web host gives you.

Did you know?

If you want to host your files, you should ask an adult for help to look for web space on a server. Just like with a Google account, you have to be a certain age to sign up.

Great work! We beat the Bond Brothers and we safely returned the Monk Diamond to Mr Volkov!

And we're famous!

WHAT NEXT?
YOUR CODING FUTURE

Over the six missions in this book, you have not only kept the Monk Diamond safe from the Bond Brothers, but have also learnt all about HTML, CSS and JavaScript. You've coded a web page, made a password, built a web-based app, planned a route and mastered some very complicated code to build a game. And now you can add creating a website to your achievements. Congratulations!

We hope Get Coding! has shown you how fun and interesting coding can be. You've learnt a truly impressive number of new Code Skills and built some exciting projects of your own. And there's still much, much more to learn. If you enjoyed coding in HTML and CSS, there are plenty of other HTML tags and CSS attributes that you can learn from lots of excellent websites on the Internet.

The W3Schools HTML site, which can be found at **www.w3schools.com/html**, will guide you through plenty of examples so you can expand your knowledge and make even more exciting websites.

If you enjoyed coding in JavaScript, why not sharpen up your skills by working through some of the exercises available on sites like Codecademy at **www.codecademy.com/learn/javascript**?

Or you could start learning new programming languages for coding programs that run outside your browser. Why not try learning C#, Java or Ruby? Or try your hand at coding your own web servers? Take a look at **www.code.org/learn** for more ideas.

And finally, don't forget to join the Young Rewired State community. We will help you to keep developing your coding skills and be a technology star of the future!

The Get Coding! missions have been a great success. It's now up to you where you go next.

Your coding future starts here!

Joining Young Rewired State

Join Young Rewired State and we will introduce you to like-minded people and expert mentors at free events all over the world, like our Festival of Code. Through us you will learn how to build apps, websites and algorithms and be inspired to use your skills to solve real world challenges.

Young Rewired State_

Find out more about Young Rewired State:
www.yrs.io   www.getcodingkids.com

INDEX

With thanks to
David Whitney, Ruth Nicholls,
Emma Mulqueeny and the
Young Rewired State ambassadors:
Alexander Craggs, Michael Cullum,
Chloe Gutteridge, Ross Kelso,
Stephen Mount, James Thompson,
Hugh Wells

First published 2016 by Walker Books Ltd
87 Vauxhall Walk, London SE11 5HJ

8 10 9 7

Written by David Whitney

Text © 2016 Young Rewired State
Illustrations © 2016 Duncan Beedie

The right of Young Rewired State and Duncan Beedie to be identified as author and illustrator respectively of this work has been asserted
by them in accordance with the Copyright, Designs and Patents Act 1988

This book has been typeset in Futura and Bokka

Printed in China

British Library Cataloguing in Publication Data:
a catalogue record for this book is available from the British Library

ISBN 978-1-4063-6684-6

www.walker.co.uk
www.getcodingkids.com